ALAIN LEROY LOCKE

Race, Culture, and the Education of African American Adults

VIBS

Volume 133

Robert Ginsberg
Founding Editor

Peter A. Redpath
Executive Editor

Associate Editors

a volume in
African American Philosophy
AFAM
J. Everet Green, Editor

Alain Leroy Locke
1886 - 1954

ALAIN LEROY LOCKE

Race, Culture, and the Education of African American Adults

Rudolph Alexander Kofi Cain

Rodopi

Amsterdam - New York, NY 2004

The paper on which this book is printed meets the requirements of "ISO 9706:1994, Information and documentation - Paper for documents - Requirements for permanence".

Second edition, 2004

ISBN: 90-420-0833-4
©Editions Rodopi B.V., Amsterdam - New York, NY 2003
Printed in the Netherlands

To my maternal grandmother, Mary Elizabeth White Branch (deceased), affectionately called Nanny, who always encouraged me to become what I am capable of becoming, and other ancestors who maintained a constant vigil of spiritual support.

To those stalwart African American philosophers and others who are committed to preserving the intellectual legacy of Alain Leroy Locke.

CONTENTS

LIST OF ILLUSTRATIONS

EDITORIAL FOREWORD

Congratulations to Rudolph Alexander Kofi Cain are in order for the first published contribution in the Value Inquiry Book Series's special series on African
American Philosophy. This text is significant for a number of reasons. It is
about the philosophical ideas of one of the most renowned Black intellectuals
and quite possibly the most highly regarded academic philosopher of African
heritage in North America. Over the past ten years we have seen a steady rise in
interest in African American philosophy and particularly the life and thoughts
of Alain Leroy Locke. This interest in Locke has gathered momentum primarily because of the indefatigable effort of philosophers like Leonard Harris,
Tommy Lott, Jeffrey Stewart, and Johnny Washington.

In 1996 and 1997, I had the privilege of organizing two conferences in
Suffern, New York, and New York City, respectively, in an attempt to situate
Locke as a past master whose thought now serves as a beacon in the emerging
Black Enlightenment. What is even more significant about this text is its critical examination of one of Locke's most important contributions to American
society, which was his life-long interest in the promotion of adult education.
Locke was convinced that there could not be social peace and economic pros-
perity unless the populace was educated. To be at ease in the world, one has to
be involved in a continuous process of education which would include a cross-
cultural or inter-cultural component and an emphasis that values pluralism in
the pursuit of world citizenship. Indeed, the twenty-first century will be Locke's
century as the centrifugal forces of economic globalization, the rapid development in telecommunications, and the depletion of natural resources, will force
the peoples of the world into greater cultural exchange and a more sophisti-
cated understanding of cultural citizenship and an enlightened cosmopolitan-
ism. In this regard, Locke was ahead of his time, and Cain has demonstrated
here that we have ignored this gentle bard to our own peril.

Robert Ginsberg, executive editor of VIBS, is to be commended for
considering this special series on African American philosophy, and we are
indebted to Rudolph Alexander Kofi Cain for calling to our attention this
highly important development of educational theory in the life and work of
Alain Leroy Locke.

J. Everet Green
Co-Editor, African American Philosophy
Associate Editor, VIBS

GUEST FOREWORD

Locke's pragmatic approach to knowledge considers learning a process. Thus, the process of learning is itself edifying. From Locke's account, "The movement for adult education among any disadvantaged group must have a dynamic and enthusiasm-compelling drive, beyond the mere literacy level, enlarging horizons and broadening human values must dominate it or the movement will stall."[1] The learners and the object of knowledge are entwined in a web of engagement. Literacy, technical skills, and intellectual strategies are not forms of knowing that are independent from the roles they play in our lives. How we learn as adults is as important as what we learn and why we learn.

Locke appreciated that learning for a disadvantaged community was far from being a value neutral activity. It is an activity that is deeply associated with the need for individual and group uplift. The motivation for learning, and thereby enthusiasm, is often a matter of individuals needing to enhance their sense of self-esteem, gaining knowledge of value for managing the travels of daily life, learning about the heroic struggles of the downtrodden, or discussing the burning issues of the day. High cultural form is not considered a good in and of itself, nor is "art for art's sake" analogously considered a good in and of itself by Locke after the demise of the Harlem Renaissance in the mid 1930s. Locke offers an appreciation for a democratic rather than aristocratic approach to all forms of edification by his 1950 "Frontiers of Culture" where he contended that we should "propagate culture democratically, to permeate ordinary living, to root it in the soil of group life."[2] Cultural expression may be contextual, but its best performativity is a contextual expression that proffers themes, idioms, styles, and messages that are universalizable. In this sense, specificity is simultaneously cosmopolitan.

Rudolph Alexander Kofi Cain provides a detailed and substantive account of Locke's philosophy of adult education, his role in developing adult education, and Locke's unique positions in a world of competing conceptions of human development. There were important debates regarding the appropriate content of adult education in a culturally pluralistic society. One such debate concerned the role of culturally specific content in adult education. In addition, there were controversies regarding the most effective methods for increasing participation by adult learners. As a secular project, some thinkers occasionally considered the lack of church participation as a programmatic failure because African Americans were most often associated with a church. The study of African American history and contributions was often considered inappropriate because it was too often wrongly believed that African Americans did not have a history of meritorious character. Thus, even if authors favored a content-inclusive adult education, they might consider the inclusion of or a focus on

African American realities inappropriate. Moreover, assimilationists, whether politically conservative or revolutionary radicals, often considered inclusion of African American realities inappropriate because it would be unnecessarily divisive by focusing inordinately on one group rather than the commonalities of all persons. Not only does Cain invite us into these debates, but he also enables us to see how Locke weaves a justification for the study of what was then known as Negro life and history. That weaving required an account that would convince the American Association for Adult Education of the merit of learning culturally specific information as well as technically useful skills. In addition, the justification had to convince funding agencies that it was in the global interest of all Americans to learn of, and address, the reality of cultural diversity and the problematic issue of race.

Cain explores the symbiotic relationships between such luminaries as Ira Reid, W.E.B. DuBois, Booker T. Washington, and Locke. He reveals how Locke's extraordinary method of pluralism and conceptual synthesis allowed Locke to have important similarities to various leaders; yet, freed him to develop a uniquely global perspective. Cain thus argues for a new way of appreciating Locke's position in American history.

Cain offers us a way of defining and conceiving Locke's approach to education, which is conceptualized as andragogy. The latter presupposes a set of assumptions about how adults learn as opposed to pedagogy, which focuses on how youth learn. Cain contends that Locke was an andragogue in the sense that he recognized that adult education required alternative instructional methods and materials other than those utilized in conventional pedagogy. Cain notes that Locke provided three reasons as evidence to support the compelling need for adult education: (1) youth education alone is insufficient to sustain one in adulthood; (2) recurrent education is necessary to keep pace with changing world conditions; and (3) the demands of an ever increasing technological society required adaptation of new strategies for living. Cain thus interprets Locke in a way that allows for important considerations that usually escape discussion. Moreover, the needs and learning styles of adults differ from young learners. Locke's approach takes this into account. Cain argues in favor of Locke's approach to teaching adults and advocates the implementation of audio and visual aids, particularly in the education of African Americans. He begins by presenting an explication of andragogy according to the formulation of Malcolm Knowles, and builds upon this concept with Locke's writings to argue for an African centered approach to African American adult education that is not plagued by ethnocentricity and demagoguery. Instead, Cain's interpretation reveals strong reasons to see that Locke offers theoretical and practical guidance needed to help transform current global patterns of violent ethnic-value strife. In particular, Locke recognized that unity does not require uniformity, that tolerance requires appreciation and knowledge rather than ignorance of others.

The exploration of Locke's contributions to adult education takes us on an intellectual sojourn through rarely traveled historical territory. Cain expands the boundaries of adult education to include topics of substantive interest to adults and not just tectonics of primary skills; he allows us to enter relatively virgin territory. In so doing, Cain points out little known debates and under-scores their relevance for modern discourse.

Leonard Harris
Purdue University

AUTHOR'S PREFACE

Over ten years ago I discovered a copy of Leonard Harris's ground-breaking work, *Philosophy Born of Struggle*, an anthology containing selected essays by distinguished African American philosophers, including Cornell West, Lucius Outlaw, Angela Davis, Bernard Boxill, Johnny Washington, and Alain Leroy Locke. The book served as a rude awakening for me because my academic training had been almost totally void of any real and meaningful exposure to the scholarship of black philosophy pacemakers. My undergraduate and graduate education had barely introduced me to some of the more classical European philosophers such as Aristotle and Plato. Subsequently, however, my developing interest in this growing and uncharted area of critical inquiry was further heightened by Johnny Washington's work, *Alain Locke and Philosophy: A Quest for Cultural Pluralism*, which includes the essay, "Educating the Masses," an incisive analysis of Locke's philosophy of education generally and adult mass education, specifically.

The journey of enlightenment for me began with a visit for a week of intensive preliminary research at the Moorland-Spingarn Research Center at Howard University, where the bulk of Locke's papers pertinent to his work in adult education was stored, but not completely catalogued. Esme Bhan, a research associate at that time, and an avid Locke scholar, guided me enthusiastically through the archival repositories. Afterward, the preparatory work undertaken at Moorland-Spingarn led me to the Special Collections division of the Schomburg Center for Research in Black Culture and the Butler Library, Columbia University, where the relevant papers on the American Association for Adult Education were catalogued in the Carnegie Corporation files. Numerous telephone contacts and written correspondence to very interested and supportive staff at the Auburn Avenue Research Library on African American History and Culture, Atlanta-Fulton Library, followed. Concurrently, a trail of letters of inquiry to persons who may have been familiar with Locke's work in adult education related projects was facilitated. This august group included Lois Mailou Jones, artist, and Richard Long, professor, Graduate Institute of the Liberal Arts, Emory University.

As the research proceeded, I was extremely fortunate to have had the opportunity to interview several individuals who shared personal recollections of Locke. I am very appreciative of the profound interest and insights, particularly the anecdotal reflections provided by Esther and James (Jack) Jackson and the late Jean Blackwell Hutson, which presented a mirror into the "manner of man."

Thus, this critical inquiry examines Locke's axiology and his philosophy of cultural pluralism and ultimately the impact of his grounding in philosophy as he became increasingly immersed in the adult education movement during the 1920s and well into the 1940s, and, most significantly, his noteworthy contributions to transforming and expanding the mission and scope of an evolving profession. In addition, his work establishes a contrasting linkage between the educational philosophies of Booker T. Washington and W.E.B. DuBois. The research concludes with a general analysis of the application of Locke's philosophical views on cultural pluralism to issues associated with current "culture wars."

This book would not have been realized without the support and assistance of numerous individuals and institutions. In addition to providing expert research assistance, Esme Bhan was continually encouraging and supportive. I extend profound gratitude to Mary Yearwood of the Schomburg Center for Research in Black Culture, Earl Banks and Sharon Robinson of the Auburn Avenue Research Library on African American History and Culture, and the staff of the Butler Library, Columbia University. I am especially indebted to David DuBois, Director of the W.E.B. DuBois Institute, Harvard University, for permission to reproduce the entire text of "The American Negro Creed." Again, I owe a debt of gratitude and appreciation to Leonard Harris and Johnny Washington, professors of philosophy at Purdue University and Southeastern Missouri State University, respectively. They saw merit in the project and willingly critiqued the manuscript draft, and offered meticulous and thoughtful, constructive comments. I thank a host of colleagues and friends whose nurturing, editorial feedback and spiritual anchoring enabled me to see the work to completion. They include Ethel Bowles, who skillfully and competently typed the initial draft of the book, Dorothy Burnham, Joyce Hansen Nelson, Emil Moxey, Curtis Lyles, Samuel Silling, and Mae Mallory. I will be forever grateful to Johnny Wilbert Smith, who performed the herculean task of word processing a revised draft of the manuscript, and exercised a tremendous amount of tolerance and patience as I struggled to adhere to editorial guidelines. I remain indebted to Leslie Gales and Doris Rowley-Hoyte, who performed the task of crisis intervention when Johnny Smith became ill. The research support from the Empire State College Foundation and the United University Professionals, and the technical assistance of Kirk Starczewski and his staff in the Office of College Relations, and the patience and information processing expertise of Janet Jones in the Office of Central Services, were critical to the successful completion of this project.

The frontispiece photograph of Alain Leroy Locke and the remaining photographs were reproduced from the Schomburg Collection at the Schomburg Center for Research in Black Culture. Permission to use these photographs was duly obtained from the New York City Public Library/Research Libraries. The Atlanta Experiment photography was taken from the Annie L. McPheeters Collection at the Auburn Avenue Research Library on African American Culture and History. Permission to use it was granted by the Atlanta-Fulton Public Library System.

One
INTRODUCTION

Alain Leroy Locke, whose name was originally Arthur Locke, was born on 13 September 1886 in Philadelphia, Pennsylvania. The only child of relatively moderate middle-class parents, Locke seemed destined to leave a mark on society because of an innate inclination toward academic prowess and a home environment which nurtured his early educational training. His access to educational institutions of the highest caliber was a manifestation and result of superb academic preparation.

Locke's father was a graduate of Howard University Law School, yet ended up working in the Philadelphia Post Office, a not-so-uncommon experience for many African Americans during post-Reconstruction in the United States. Locke's father had impeccable credentials, having worked as the Secretary for General O. O. Howard, director of the Freedmen's Bureau, and taught mathematics to emancipated slaves in North Carolina. Locke's mother, a devoted teacher in the Camden, New Jersey, school system, assumed total responsibility for raising Locke following his father's death when Alain was six years old.

Locke has been described as a child who had to overcome the constraints imposed by rheumatic fever, which resulted in irreparable damage to his heart. According to David Levering Lewis, "convinced that he had a bad heart and an unappealing physical appearance, there was little left to Locke but to win the world's indulgence through intellectual excellence."[1] As a compensatory response to limitations growing out of bouts with his illness, he was exposed to a broad range of classical literature, and at an early age became an avid reader. Douglass Stafford poignantly notes that Locke was "a precocious child . . . the earlier years did more to shape the vain tenor of his work than usually guessed," [the assumption being that the exposure to Harvard scholars . . . including William James and George Santayana, had the greatest impact].[2] Stafford continues, "to probe cautiously into the influences surrounding his childhood may unfold naturally the growth of his thought and feeling."

Locke attended the Ethical Culture School, where he excelled; went on to high school and graduated second in his class; studied for two years at the Philadelphia School of Pedagogy, ultimately graduating first in his class. Locke was admitted to Harvard College in 1904 and completed a four-year program in three years. He was inducted into Phi Beta Kappa at Harvard. A noteworthy first is Locke's selection as a Rhodes Scholar, after having completed his work at Harvard College. This prestigious accomplishment was not to be without some political ramifications. Although the Rhodes scholarship was to provide an opportunity for this fledgling African American scholar to study philosophy at Oxford University, Rayford Logan makes the following observation:

Locke rebuffed by five (5) Oxford Colleges, which under agreement establishing the Rhodes Scholarship retain the right of admissions, was admitted to Hertford College, where he studied Philosophy, Greek and *Literae Humaniores* from 1907 to 1910.[3]

After completing his work at Hertford, described by Leonard Harris as "one of the youngest and poorest" colleges in the Oxford system, and as one of the least academically strong Oxford Colleges, Locke spent one year at the University of Berlin.[4] Racism no doubt played a pivotal role in Locke's rejection by some of the more prestigious Oxford Colleges, and that elements of xenophobia and in Lockean terms, "Negrophobia," were significant operating variables. For here was one of our "talented tenth" who had been academically groomed for the challenge, yet had become a victim of DuBois's prediction that the problem of the twentieth century would ultimately be that of color.

Harris notes the transatlantic depth of racism when he observed that Locke had not been invited to a Thanksgiving dinner in 1907 sponsored by Americans to honor Rhodes Scholars.[5] The white southern scholars had successfully launched a collective effort to exclude him. This indignity prompted Horace M. Kallen, a noted American philosopher, to boycott the event.

Kallen, who was at Oxford during Locke's tenure (1907-1910), observed the following:

> I know that at Oxford — I was there at the time — he was penalized. There were among the Rhodes scholars at Oxford, gentlemen from Dixie who could not possibly associate with Negroes. They could not possibly attend the Thanksgiving dinner celebrated by Americans if a Negro was to be there. So although students from elsewhere in the United States outnumbered the gentlemen from Dixie, Locke was not invited; and one or two other persons, authentically Americans, refused in consequence to attend.[6]

Little did Locke know or expect that such encounters would consciously or subconsciously impact on his evolution as a scholar, and that the subsequent development of his philosophical ideas would reverberate themes of racial and cultural integrity which encouraged diversity within the context of global understanding.

In his *Race Contacts and Interracial Relations*, Locke exposes and analyzes a broad range of insights that focus on the theme of value conflicts among individuals and groups. He held that color is less important than economic and political inequity as catalysts for racial conflict. As we witness continuing ethnic/racial conflict on a global level, it might be instructive to revisit some of Locke's philosophical and anthropological perspectives.

Locke was an idealist and a visionary. However, American culture has simply not evolved as Locke had hoped and predicted. The ideal society is nowhere to be seen in America today. Most of our schools remain segregated by geography, economic status, and custom. A similar situation of *de facto* segregation exists in residential housing. Ethnic and racial groups remain socially isolated. Although the economic and political conditions of African Americans may have improved over the centuries, the control and power of the political and economic systems remain in the hands of whites. The use of cultural education as a mechanism for political and economic awakening and empowerment seems a valid way of reducing the extent of racial conflict. Unfortunately, this approach has resulted in the exploitation, commercialization, and ultimate control of the culture of the African American community. Two cases in point are African American art and music, once considered less than aesthetically acceptable. Yet, on many levels these artistic forms, once validated by whites, became more marketable; and they are largely controlled economically by whites.

In keeping with his resolve to secure aesthetic parity in mainstream white America for the artistic works of African Americans, Locke actively sought to address the issue in the academic arena.

Upon his return from studying in Europe, he joined the faculty of Teachers College at Howard University as Professor of Education and Philosophy. Following four years of teaching at Howard, Locke received a fellowship to complete doctoral studies in philosophy at Harvard University. In 1918, he was awarded the Doctor of Philosophy degree and resumed his teaching career at Howard University, with which he established a lifelong relationship, though it was often characterized by controversy. One example is the incident in which he and others were fired by Howard University on the grounds of reorganization needs, though Locke was subsequently rehired as Chair of the Philosophy Department. Leonard Harris hypothesizes an alternate reason for the firing purge — "to reduce the power of forces pursuing equitable pay between blacks and whites, the Howard University administration fired Locke in June of 1925, along with several other black faculty members."[7]

As he challenged the labor practices of Howard, Locke embarked on an academic mission aimed at incorporating African Studies and Race Relations in the curriculum, thus signifying an extension and application of some of his pivotal philosophical conceptions. Harris observes the following:

> Although enamored at a young age by the lifestyle of classical Greek culture, educated at institutions offering little positive incentive to study African culture or race relations, and also attracted to the spirituality of the Bahai [the unity of religions], Locke felt that the promotion and study of African Culture and race relations were integral to his being. In 1915 and 1916 he fought to offer a course on race relations against the wishes of the Howard University Administration. The administration denied him the opportunity to offer the course in its curriculum, but he eventually

taught the course to a study group under the aegis of the National Association for the Advancement of Colored People (N.A.A.C.P.).[8]

Although Locke was trained in the field of philosophy, he is not known
for his proliferation of philosophical treatises. His essay on "Values and Imperatives" and his Ph.D. dissertation topic, "The Problem of Classification in
the Theory of Values," received the most attention in the literature. As Johnny
Washington notes, "the most pervasive theme in his works is the value conflicts among individuals and groups."[9] He adds, "Values and Imperatives," for
instance, "illuminated the sources from which such conflicts arose and offered
the means of reducing them." In his role as an adult educator and leader in the
adult education movement, Locke advocated the pivotal importance of cultural
studies in adult education as one remedy for value conflicts.

Harris makes the following observation, which provides some further insights into Lockean educational philosophy:

> The study of cultural subjects in mass education is important not only
> because of their intellectual value, but also because such subjects insure
> learners to acquire knowledge. Locke maintained that this element of
> inspiration was especially important for Blacks who had been damaged
> psychologically and spiritually by the conditions of oppression. If the Black
> masses were not inspired to acquire education through the study of cul-
> tural subjects, their education would be a failure.[10]

Locke, like Hannah Arendt, Jean-Paul Sartre, and others, sought to relate
philosophy to practical affairs. However, unlike Arendt and Sartre, Locke was
greatly pragmatic: he was very concerned with the everyday lives of African
Americans and actively sought to improve the quality and conditions of their
lives. Indeed, Locke personifies the description of Cornel West's characterization
of an "intellectual" as opposed to a "scholar." As an intellectual, West[11] envi-
sions a person motivated by social reality and social change, as contrasted with
the scholar, who narrowly engages in scholarly endeavors.

As was mentioned, Locke's writing consistently reverberated philosophical themes, most often touching upon global justice and tolerance and race and
ethnic relations. Locke's own sense of a worldview or global perspective is
well captured in the following:

> In terms of the race question as a world problem, the Negro mind has
> leapt, so to speak, upon the parapets of prejudice and extended its cramped
> horizons. In doing so it has linked up with the growing group conscious-
> ness of the dark-peoples and is gradually learning their common interests.
> As one of our writers has recently put it: "It is imperative that we under-
> stand the white world in its relations to the non-white world." As with the

Jew, persecution is making the Negro international. As a world phenomenon this wider race consciousness is a different thing from the much asserted rising tide of color. Its inevitable causes are not of our making, the consequences are not necessarily damaging to the best interests of civilization whether it actually brings into being new armadas of conflict or argosies of cultural change and enlightenment can only be decided by the attitude of the dominant race in an era of critical change.[12]

Locke's contributions to adult education in this country were thus grounded in his philosophical theories. Among other observations, he noted that pluralism may serve to give meaning to differential modes of valuing and that cultural relativism can function as an antidote to inequality and social injustice. Yet Locke's sterling contributions to the adult education movement have typically been overlooked in favor of his involvement and leadership in the Harlem Renaissance. Richard Long, for instance, insists, "it is no exaggeration to say that the Harlem Renaissance as we know it is marked strongly by the presence of Alain Locke and would have been something rather different without the role of mentor which he filled with modesty and elegance."[13]

Elinor Des Verney Sinnette points out that as a member of the Negro Society for Historical Research, Locke advocated "first, that the race problem existed not only in the United States and the Caribbean but throughout the world and wherever Blacks were to be found; and, second, the Blacks would do well to give more serious considerations to their African heritage as the foundation of their history and culture."[14] Academics and practitioners in the field, as well as lay persons, often fail to recognize Locke's profound impact on transforming the field of adult education, which is the focus of this work.

Locke played a key role in bringing attention to the need for the mass education of African Americans who as a group were not far removed from enslavement, and confronted with the adverse conditions brought on by migration to primarily large urban centers. Locke further insisted on greater inclusion of African Americans in services and programs, whether as providers or recipients. Yet, several core books in the field make little or no reference to Locke. Malcolm Knowles's benchmark work, an historiography of the adult education movement, makes only a passing reference to the Bronze Booklets, a major legacy of Locke's leadership of the Association for Negro Folk Education, and a project enthusiastically supported by the American Association for Adult Education, the Rosenwald Fund, and the Carnegie Corporation.[15] A subsequent and very impressive piece of research on African American adult education by Harvey G. Neufeldt and Leo McGee cite several programs under Locke's stewardship, but fails to provide a clear delineation of his role.[16] Harold Stubblefield's work, another historical portrayal of the adult education movement, makes no reference to Locke in spite of the fact that he devotes a significant portion of his work to "Adult Education as social education,"[17] an important dimension of

Locke's philosophical formulations and perspectives on adult education. One of the most recent articles to be published about Locke and his work in adult education appeared over eighteen years ago, authored by Robert Hayden and Eugene DuBois.[18] Two doctoral dissertations have been written during the past seventeen years. Everett Alston Days's work, "Alain Leroy Locke (1886-1954): Pioneer in Adult Education and Catalyst in the Adult Education Movement for Black Americans," focuses on Locke's major contributions from a concretely programmatic perspective.[19] However, absent from Days's research is the Bronze Booklet Series, considered by many to have been Locke's stellar achievement. Talmadge Carter Guy's dissertation, "Prophecy from the Periphery: Alain Locke's Philosophy of Cultural Pluralism and Adult Education," represents an in-depth critical inquiry into Locke's philosophy of adult education.[20]

Two additional works provide valuable insights about Locke's philosophy of education. Russell Linneman's collective volume contains some incisive analyses of Locke's views on values and education.[21] Johnny Washington, an African American philosopher, includes in his book an enlightening discourse on Locke's opinions on mass education.[22] Elizabeth Peterson's book contains two essays that highlight Alain Locke's involvement in adult education.[23] Though interest in Locke's adult education work is growing, continuing efforts seem warranted as we continue to confront the problem of illiteracy generally, the staggering high school drop-out rate, and increasing disparities in educational opportunity. Thus Locke's philosophy of adult education, well-expressed in the following, should be revisited:

> The quest for a common objective — the discovery of integrating elements for knowledge is the search for focalizing approaches in education . . . critical thinking . . . could make no greater headway in a single line of uncompromising advance than, with such a strategic methodology as tactic, to involve the innermost citadel of dogmatic thinking.[24]

Locke elucidated what he considered to be the purview of adult education by asserting:

> It should be fairly evident that only the systematic training of adults rather than mere informing, persuading, entertaining, or propagandizing of adults is the proper scope of any adult education worthy of the name or serious consideration.[25]

Rayford Logan and Michael Winston note, "almost concurrently with his work on the reform of Howard University's liberal arts curriculum, Locke became more deeply involved in the adult education movement in which he had first participated in 1924 as a delegate to the first adult education conference sponsored by the Carnegie Foundation."[26] Noteworthy is Locke's ascendancy to the presidency of the American Association for Adult Education in 1946, after having served on numerous occasions as a delegate and Vice President. Guy observes that Locke was elected President in absentia because of a prior commitment precluding his attendance at the annual AAAE Conference in 1946.[27] Locke became the first African American to assume this top prestigious leadership position. Consequently, his association with the American Association for Adult Education spanned more than twenty years. To a proper context in terms of Locke's association with the American Association for Adult Education, it is worthwhile to state the objective of the organization (1926-1951):

> The American Association for Adult Education was organized in 1926 to further the idea of education as a continuing process throughout life. It aims to serve as a clearinghouse for information in the field of adult education; to assist enterprises already in operation; to help organizations and groups to initiate adult education activities; to aid and advise individuals who, although occupied with some primary vocation or interest, desire to continue learning on their own.[28]

This book explores the tenets of Locke's educational philosophy and the influence of his academic training in philosophy on the evolution of his philosophical perspectives on general education and on African American adult education. Importantly, an examination of specific strategies, programmatic and operational thrusts of adult education which were advocated by Locke, are pivotal dimensions of this discourse. Locke's immersion in the adult education movement, his leadership and his advocacy of needs of African American adults, and contemporary implications will be examined in greater detail and analysis.

Although Locke's journal publications in philosophy are limited in volume, they are nevertheless profound. In this light, he is regarded as a professional philosopher. Linnemann lauds Locke's contribution to philosophical thinking, yet suggests that had Locke devoted more time and effort to the development of his philosophical ideas, he might have become one of the world's most eminent philosophers.[29] Mark Helbing provides the following insights:

> For Locke, man lives in a world of meaning, for experience itself is a qualitative act. As a consequence, Locke stresses the importance of "values" in human behavior, and not simply as moral categories or codes of conduct but rather as qualities of perception rooted in the existential nature of man himself, noting that "we must realize that not in every instance is this normative control effected indirectly through judgement or evaluational processes, but through primary mechanisms of feeling modes and dispositional attitudes."[30]

Yet, in spite of the dearth of philosophical writings and treatises, Locke practiced philosophy, and was a personification of the Socratic tradition —

referring to himself as a Socratic mid-wife. According to Harris, "between 1912 and 1954, the majority of Afro-American students of philosophy attending universities in the United States were either taught by Locke or one of the Black philosophers he was instrumental in hiring at Howard University."[31] On a broader scale, Locke's apparent Socratic character is supported by Long when he observes that "in spite of the professional demands on his time in terms of writing and teaching, Locke's active encouragement of young Black writers, artists, and scholars wherever he found them" was a striking dimension of his character.[32] Washington elucidates the Socratic tradition in the following manner:

> The state became the classroom where Socrates practiced his social philosophy and the Athenian citizens were his students. Ironically, he admitted that he had nothing to teach, no philosophic truth to impart. He admitted that, unlike the gods he was not a wise man, rather he was only insofar as he knew nothing. His teaching took the form of midwifery whereby he assisted people in espousing their ignorance, in delivering their own insights, and in re-examining their stereotyped assumptions.[33]

Locke had an abiding concern for the African American scholar's dilemma in the American democratic society. This concern is well-articulated by Eugene Holmes:

> Alain Locke possessed and professed a philosophical credo — the view of humanity that there is a uniqueness of the personality, an individuation of the psyche and the soma which are essentially communicable. This indefeasibility of the individual's experiences is physical and ethical, allowing for the development of a man's own inner personality and freedom. As a sensitive member of a minority group he saw in retrospect that the Negro scholar's ability to withstand the infirmities of the American scene is a dialectic phase of the democratic process which must necessarily aid in bringing to fruition the dream of a community of Negro scholars. This was his sensitivity about American history, and it led him to an identity with the great leader, the self-taught Frederick Douglass, and to mutual understanding, if sometimes mild controversy with W.E.B. DuBois.[34]

Another, yet more personal dimension of "the manner of the man" is described by A. Gilbert Belle:

> He was a man who chose his words carefully and tried to make them count, as he stayed clear of ineptness and shallowness. His friends remember him as one who did not waste nor engage in small talk. He attended, participated, observed, evaluated, and reported on the ongoing struggles that faced a college professor, a concerned citizen, and a freedom-conscious black man.[35]

Logan and Winston observe that Locke's "many contacts with influential white editors, scholars, philanthropists, government leaders, and patrons of the arts, gave him an unusual opportunity to foster the concerns of young writers and artists."[36] Notably this illustrious circle included Carl Van Vechten (photographer), Charlotte Mason (philanthropist), Nancy Cunard (writer and shipbuilding heiress), and Fiorello LaGuardia (Mayor of New York).

To argue that Locke's philosophical ideas influenced his approach to the education of African American adults, we should first examine the central tenets of these ideas. Two important works by Locke previously mentioned, his Ph.D. dissertation, "The Problem of Classification in the Theory of Values," and "Values and Imperatives," are appropriate contexts for a conceptualization of his philosophical ideas and insights about education generally, and the education of African American adults specifically. First, Linnemann notes that "the essence of his [Locke's] position is that values should be classified in terms of the philosophical and affective factors involved in the valuation experience."[37] What seems to evolve is a fusion of meaning and feeling about a situation or experience. Second, and perhaps more importantly, what has evolved from Locke's philosophical system of ideas of valuation is a rejection of absolutes and an embracing of value relativity and cultural pluralism.

Thus, Locke saw adult education of the masses as a vehicle for the inculcation of a values system that respected differences. He believed unrelentingly and passionately in the critical role that the teaching of culture and history plays in achieving global tolerance and understanding. Holmes reiterates Locke's belief that adult education for African Americans had to be grounded in the history and culture of this group.[38] Hayden and DuBois emphasize Locke's view that the teaching of history could generate profound "sustained interest" in adult education.[39] Washington highlights Locke's position regarding the inspirational value inherent in studying cultural subjects for both African Americans and other groups.[40] Washington also observes, "the most pervasive theme in his [Locke's] work is the value conflicts among individuals and groups."[41]

Consequently, Locke emphasized the emotional dimension of values, which was encapsulated in attitudes and feelings. Ultimately, value judgments were to be immersed in the subjective world and not reality. A deleterious result of this immersion is the subsequent emergence of stereotypes.

Locke argued that values could be indeed altered or shifted by changes in attitudes, thereby, proposing the idea that values or norms were historically, socially, and culturally determined. A classic case in point is the earlier view, which persists on some levels today, held by many white Americans that African Americans were bereft of "culture capital," resulting in the emergence of indifference and intolerance based on some type of arbitrary and capricious standard. For Locke, the imposition of such generalized standards or absolutes, was counter-productive to achieving sound race relations, tolerance and respect for differences. Thus, the Harlem Renaissance, for instance, epitomized efforts to counter the negative images of African Americans as culturally, artistically and intellectually inept. The "New Negro" symbolized efforts to legitimize artistic self-expression.

Leonard Harris explains that "The phrase 'New Negro' was used to denote the rise of black cultural characteristics warranting merit. It was marshalled to battle racist stereotypes of black people as having static, unchangeable characteristics."[42] He continues, "Given white society's entrenched belief in the inferiority of black people and that as manifest in the unworthiness of black culture, the existence of the 'New Negro' was thus at once evidence of the falsity of the stereotype and grounds for a different perception of black people and black culture."[43] Ideally, Locke and others envisioned the realization of such legitimacy as a critical step toward the inclusion of African Americans in the larger American cultural and democratic tradition. Thus, Locke favored a functionalist rather than abstract perspective on values. The functionalist perspective would serve as a corrective mode that "might correct some of our basic culture dogmatism and progressively cure many of our most intolerant and prejudicial culture attitudes and practices."[44] Locke's insistence on the functional role of values is buttressed by the following:

> one of the most important and baffling of the provinces of philosophy. Its importance as primary point of contact between thought and actual living is seldom given proper emphasis in either professional or lay thinking. The reasons are many, among them our chronic inclination to take values for granted. . . . It is both a notable and welcome exception to encounter an analysis of value that, without loss of scholarly depth, examines values in the vital context of their actual functioning, and as in the case of Realisms of Values, yields cumulative insight into the role of values in motivating and in providing sanctions — rational and rationalized — for our civilization.[45]

But what does the aforementioned have to do with Locke and adult education? Let us consider how some possible relationships between Locke's axiology and his perspectives on cultural pluralism provide some enlightenment on his views about the direction of adult education. First, the previous observations regarding the functional role of adult education are particularly pertinent. Locke believed in the primacy of life experiences for forging a transformation of the quality of living. Thus, adult education was seen as a meaningful strategic approach for reducing value conflicts among individuals and groups. Ideally, Locke had envisioned an ideal society that would respect and tolerate differences through an enhanced valuing of those differences, ultimately crumbling the walls of segregation and racism. Since the public school system in the United States had clearly failed in this respect, the result was an adult population that was both culturally illiterate and insensitive to differences. Locke believed that adult education must therefore assume the responsibility of an "unfinished democracy." Second, for Locke, the psychological casualties resulting from value conflicts on many levels of American society had taken their greatest toll on African Americans. He notes:

> It is obvious that the Negro section of the population stands deeply in need of such compensatory and inspiring materials [culturally based curriculum materials]. More than that, in addition to serving the adult group directly, education in this direction seems double. Through the influence of the present generation upon the youth, we can particularly check the artificial discouragement of the limited past of their elders and keep from adding unnecessarily to actual, situational disabilities of the young.[46]

. . .

> Indeed, there is little use in the teaching of race pride to the younger generation unless it be reinforced — and intelligently reinforced, in the attitudes of the older generations. This is a special obligation and opportunity of the adult education movement among us; and in my judgement . . . To carry it through effectively should be one of the prime objectives of our adult education work for Negroes.[47]

Readers interested in a more in-depth analysis of Alain Locke's contributions to value theory may read Locke's "Values and Imperatives," which appears in the 1935 publication *American Philosophy, Today and Tomorrow*, edited by Horace M. Kallen and Sidney Hook. Also instructive is Leonard Harris's book, *The Philosophy of Alain Locke* and Russell Linnemann's work, *Reflections on a Modern Renaissance Man*. In addition, Johnny Washington's discourse on "Alain Locke's Values and Imperatives," which appears in Harris's earlier groundbreaking work, *Philosophy Born of Struggle,* offers insightful interpretations. In chronicling and analyzing Locke's involvement in the adult education movement, it should be beneficial to formulate a broader historical context, as follows.

The adult education movement in this country took its roots following World War I. Although prior to this time a plethora of uncoordinated adult education activities existed, they lacked integration and clearly defined philosophical direction. Stubblefield observes that many institutions used these activities for a broad range of interests and needs.[48] The critical challenge during this post-war period was how best to prepare American citizens and immigrants to deal with a new social order that was accompanied by an "explosion of knowledge." In response, numerous schools of thought evolved. In his book, Stubblefield outlines three primary historical and philosophical approaches to adult education: (1) Adult Education as diffusion of knowledge; (2) Adult Education as Liberal Education; and (3) Adult Education as Social Education. The latter approach mirrors Locke's thinking and ideals about the functional role of adult education.

Malcolm Knowles's work on the historical development of adult education in the United States has become a "bible" in the field that chronicles the
movement. Essentially, Knowles outlines specific adult education program activities from colonial times to the 1960s. These activities were directly an out-
growth of existing social conditions. For instance, during the period 1780–1865,
programs that took the shape of town meetings were aimed at the Americanization of new immigrants (white Europeans) and agricultural education. Such
programs were tied to the needed economic development of a relatively new
nation. Clearly, during this period, free blacks were excluded from participation
in adult education–related activities. The exception was one work of the
Freedmen's Bureau that launched an aggressive program aimed at educating
the hundreds of thousands of free blacks. On the other hand, the period between
1886 and 1920, witnessed the founding of African American colleges and the
emergence of correspondence schools. Knowles provides the following highly
relevant backdrop:

> The big tragedy of this period was that following the Emancipation Proc-
> lamation and the ending of the Civil War, adult education was not used as
> an instrument of national policy to equip the freed slaves to enter the main
> current of American life on a massive scale — as was done a quarter of a
> century later with the waves of European immigrants.[49]

We should acknowledge the extraordinary work of such organizations as
the Freedmen's Bureau during this period. Yet, Knowles cautions that these and
other such efforts fell far short of the need.

During the 1920s to the 1960s, churches became prominent institutions in
providing broadly defined educational opportunities for adults. The Post 1960s
was a period of increasing involvement of community colleges, labor unions,
and similar such organizations. Regrettably, Knowles's standard history of the
American adult education movement devotes little space to the African American agenda, with the exception of a brief mention of the education of ex-slaves
and the promotion of educational activities of the National Association for the
Advancement of Colored People and the Urban League. Fortunately for us,
Neufeldt and McGee have made an earnest effort to fill the gap.[50]

Unfortunately, Locke is mentioned only on two pages of above cited text,
while in Knowles's book, no mention is made. Thus, in an ironic twist, one
might view Locke as a posthumous victim of his own axiology — the idea that
values represent personal attitudes about what is worthy or not worthy. In consideration of Locke's stellar record of over twenty years of devoted service to
such a mass movement as adult education, one would expect the literature to
abound with significant references to his work. Lamentably, the blatant ab-
sence of the contributions of African Americans in other realms of the social
history of America continues on many levels to be the rule rather than the exception, thus posing a more universal question of what and how we value.

The thrust of adult education during the 1970s and 1980s focused on recurrent and life-long learning education accented with the appearance of new technologies used in the delivery of educational services.

Defining adult education has been a challenge in efforts to plot the direction of the adult education movement, some very general and all-encompassing in meaning, and others more specific in broadening the intrinsic scope of the field. For instance, Knowles makes a distinction between a broad and technical meaning.[51] In the first instance, he talks about a "process" of continuing and recurrent education, an idea fostered by the American Association for Adult Education during its infancy. In the second, he emphasizes a set of organized activities such as lecture series. Thus, meaning and definition may have been recurrent issues.

Stubblefield found that underlying many of the definitions of adult education was the question/argument, "How persons should be trained to live in American culture."[52] He surmises that "the term adult education was widely used as the covering term for a wide variety of activities that served propaganda and profit-making as well as educational purposes."[53] He continues by observing that "many persons used the term adult education as a label for their activities simply because the term was in vogue [after World War I]. They were unaware of any deeper and non-institutional meaning that the term might have had."[54] Thus, academics, professionals, and practitioners focused on formulating definitions that provided coherence and meaningful purpose. For instance, Lyman Bryson viewed adult education as "all the activities with an educational purpose that are carried on by people engaged in the ordinary business of life."[55] On the other hand, Long argues that "in the broadest sense, education of adults can be used to include all systematic efforts to obtain knowledge,"[56]

Others were specific in infusing more globally intrinsic values. Eduard Lindeman, a pioneer in advocating adult education as social action, defined adult education as "individual growth through learning in social medium for social end."[57] Locke was tremendously influenced by Lindeman because of his emphasis on social and cultural imperatives aimed at addressing such critical areas as race relations. Finally, Locke, an early critic of the failure of the movement to define its purpose and direction, posits the following definition:

> It should be fairly evident that only the systematic training of adults rather than the mere informing, persuading, entertaining or propagandizing of adults is the proper scope of any adult education worthy of any serious consideration.[58]

He expanded and refined his point by noting:

> It should never be forgotten that "education" is the substance of the matter and "adult" merely the adjectival reference. Adult education effort may

be as informed, as uncertified, as untechnical as permitted by the subject matter, as many-sided as life experience itself, but it must be at least systematic, standardized, and expertly administered or, whatever else it is (and however useful), it is not entitled to be called "adult education."[59]

Locke was a proponent of more intrinsic values for adult education, probably influenced by his training in philosophy. Linnemann clarifies Locke's explanation of intrinsic values by noting:

Locke had in mind those vital functional norms that sustain existence, or its "vital mode of living." This involves basically the manner in which a culture structures reality on the things in nature in order to make sense of the world. It involves, in short, understanding man [and woman] racially and culturally.[60]

Holmes observes, "Alain Locke perhaps deserves the honor of being the first Negro [African American] educator to recognize the intrinsic value of adult education which at the same time would provide a scientific basis for all adults as well as being a vital instrument for their social advancement."[61] Locke's perspectives enhanced a global outlook:

Our obligation is obvious; our chances of making constructive international contributions is challenging. The core problem of our field today is therefore the development of most effective techniques of mass education, bold and pioneering experimentation with the new mass media of communication to make them serve the social and cultural needs of even larger and larger segments of people. By radio, motion picture, and visual materials of all sorts, the adult education radius of teaching and propaganda must extend to the new dimensions of human interest and values, fresh emphasis on the social aspects and implications of knowledge and deeper concern with personal and group attitudes than with mere informational knowledge or individual skills.[62]

Thus, Locke's vision for adult education seems to have preceded the proliferation in the 1960s of a broad range of non-traditional educational service delivery systems that rely significantly on alternative teaching methods and a vast array of communications technology: radio, television, mass book production, programmed instructions, xerography, audiotapes, microfilm and microfiche, computer assisted instruction, and cable television. The Information Superhighway offers unlimited possibilities for mass global education. The central question — one that Locke would likely raise — is, "Who will benefit from these broad leaps in educational technology?" Also, Locke's concern about the social implications of informational knowledge seems warranted as we witness the escalation of ethnic and racial conflict on a global scale. Will increased advances in educational technology serve to address the problems of the human condition?

In the case of African Americans, Locke believed that advances in science and technology had eradicated socially constructed differences:

> In spite of the leveling off of many present differences under the impact of science, technology, and increased intercommunications, we cannot in any reasonably near future envisage any substantial lessening of the differences in our basic value systems, either philosophical or cultural. The only viable alternative seems, therefore, not to expect to change others but to change our attitudes toward them, and to seek reproachment not by the eradication of such differences as there are but by schooling ourselves not to make so much of differences. These differences, since they are as real and hard as "facts" should be accepted as unemotionally and objectively as we accept fact.[63]

Locke was ever vigilant in exposing the paradox between the rhetoric of democracy and its failure to "deliver on the promise" of freedom and equality for all. Certainly, for Locke, education was a significant dimension of that premise, since participation in the democratic process required an enlightened constituency. For Locke, extending these rights and privileges to groups historically denied such rights had been too long delayed. Guy observes that "during the last fifteen years of his life, Locke's writings and activities shifted focus to issues having more to do with the problems of democracy and minorities."[64] That is, Locke realized that cultural appreciation alone could not take precedence over certain stark ideological and political realities.

Consequently, in numerous instances Locke challenged the leadership of AAAE to assume a more proactive role in creating programs that would, for instance, address social and political oppression. Though on some levels of the leadership a shared commitment existed, most endorsed a narrow vision of adult education that did not particularly embrace social and political change. However, Locke persisted in his view that the crisis in education inextricably mirrored the crisis in American democracy. Consequently, as Guy observes, "Locke's interest in intercultural understanding and parity among groups, framed his own method of working out an answer to the problems."[65] Furthermore, Locke cautioned the leadership of the AAAE:

> The movement for adult education among any disadvantaged group must have a dynamic and enthusiasm – compelling drive. Beyond the literacy level, enlarging horizons and broadening human values must dominate it or the movement will stall. It can never be successful in terms of the surface scratching of remedial programs designed to remove handicaps.[66]

Locke's approach to reconstructing and reintegrating the educational system within the context of underlying democratic principles, are practical and at times poetically articulated. His invocation of a medicine analogy is ingenious. He envisioned the school (including and extending to adult education programs) as a laboratory for "sterilizing the emotional beds of pride and prejudice, realizing that not all pride is healthy, and that the variety which is founded upon the depreciation of other groups and thrives at their expense is unsound and dangerous."[67] Then, in his speech accepting the Presidency of the American Association for Adult Education, Locke shared the sentiments of William Townsend who said that "adult education must be functional and not an ornamental mantelpiece in the field of democratic education." The Townsend excerpt used by Locke was:

> For it is only by being functional that it can render great service to the democratic aspirations of the common people. It should stand for something more important in our lives than just a hobby club or sewing circle. It is this hobby-lobby, sewing-circle philosophy of adult education that permeates the movement and is largely responsible for its acute inferiority complex. However, there are brave souls who desire to break through the maze of the many inconsequential activities of adult education; and these are the pioneers who will conquer the new social frontiers.[68]

Locke profoundly shared the sentiments of Townsend. As Johnny Washington notes, Locke "claimed that in order to improve the conditions of blacks and promote the spread of democracy generally, society must educate the masses, especially blacks who for centuries had been denied adequate education."[69] Locke, himself, observed that "Democracy itself is obstructed and stagnated to the extent that any of its channels are closed. So the choice is not between one way for the Negro and another way for the rest, but between American institutions frustrated on the one hand and American ideals progressively fulfilled and realized on the other."[70] Consequently, he formulated a direct link between extrinsic and intrinsic values in adult education:

> To reach any considerable measure of individual success without equally defined social objectives seems quite quixotic and futile. For in the long run we must measure effective adult education in most cases by its social or mass results.[71]

His call for broadening the scope of adult education is captured in the following:

> If we envisage a democratic national situation at all, we must hope to see all special and separate programs of mass education, such as community projects, worker's education, basic programs of publicly supported adult education. This, too, is not only in the interest of the proper integration of

the Negro clientele, but for a properly democratic background of experience for all members of a truly democratic society. Having to get one's adult education in a fully democratic social context may, after all, be the most importantly educative common aspect of the whole experience.[72]

Locke's immersion in the adult education movement was not self-initiated. As a prominent African American intellectual, he was recruited by the leadership at a time when the adult education movement was struggling to establish some degree of legitimacy and credibility, and attempting to counter any image of the movement as being exclusionary. As Sinnette observes, Locke "spent as much of his non-teaching time as possible in New York,"[73] serving as a member of the Advisory Committee of the Harlem Experiment, a community adult education program which was supported by the Carnegie Corporation, the Rosenwald Fund, and the American Association for Adult Education. The program, which ran for three years, was based at the 135th Street branch of the New York Public Library, the mecca for the Harlem Renaissance. Locke was a cardinal shaker and mover of this African American – centered, historical, cultural and artistic movement of the 1920s, which left an indelible legacy of African American cultural and intellectual thought, and significantly helped to define and shape the African American aesthetic in what was to be conceptualized by Locke as the "New Negro."[74] It will hopefully become apparent in this volume that Locke's African American – centeredness influenced his adult education work.

Because of Locke's influence, along with that of James Weldon Johnson, W.E.B. DuBois, and others, David Levering Lewis refers to Locke as "The Proust of Lenox Avenue."[75] Steven Watson captures Locke's principal role in the Harlem Renaissance Movement when he notes:

> Seen as an artist manque and a writer of real if not profound ability, Locke's chief contribution to the Harlem Renaissance was catalyzing others and crystallizing the ideas about the New Negro. Interweaving many skeins — African and European, classical and contemporary — Locke became the young movement's most articulate voice, its precious oracle, and the official mentor to its new recruits.[76]

Lewis further characterizes Locke as the "impresario" of the movement. I would add that Locke's view was that African American art had to be transformed from its American-centeredness to a level of African-centeredness. Therefore, he encouraged the African American artist to accept the challenge of recapturing the spiritual and aesthetic legacy of his/her African ancestral heritage. Also, in the tradition of Molefi Asante's Africentric idea, in many respects, the Harlem Renaissance challenged the imposition of the white supremacist view as universal or "classical," and thus, was the kernel of a major effort to reclaim a cultural past rooted in African tradition.[77]

Symbolically, Locke's baptism in the adult education movement occurred in 1932, when he accepted an invitation from the Carnegie Corporation to evaluate the Harlem and Atlanta Experiments in adult education. Growing out of the experience of having evaluated these two experimental programs for African American adult learners, Locke predicted that "history and culture [the thrust of the experimental programs] would not only stimulate interest but would also, in time" provide for mass adult education in black communities.[78]

Locke's active involvement in the adult education movement spanned a period of over twenty years. Following his death in 1954, the *New York Times* reported, "through his addresses and his writing, Locke acquired a reputation as one of the leading interpreters of the cultural achievement of the Negro, and as one of the wisest analysts of his race and its relations with other races."[79] Though the obituary made no specific reference to adult education and his substantial contributions to the movement, several significant works associated with his work in adult education were cited — *The Negro and His Music* and *The Negro in Art,* two pivotal works in the Bronze Booklet Series.

A litany of crowning testimonials to his scholarship and intellectual acumen characterized the tone of his funeral, which was held in New York City on 11 June 1954, was published in *Phylon*.[80] Ralph Bunche had supported many of Locke's adult education-related activities and shared his globalist perspectives. Locke had been a "friend and mentor" to Bunche during Bunche's student days at Howard University. Bunche, who later was to become the first African American Undersecretary of the United Nations, noted: "Philosopher he was; thinker and writer; and intellectual; a man of conviction with courage of conviction."[81] William Brathwaite, Harlem Renaissance writer, made reference to Locke's globalist perspectives by observing that "he saw beyond the local, and detached the universal spirit of man, and sought to bring these segments of social and economic differences into a universal spiritual balance."[82] Then, Benjamin Karpman, philosopher, underscoring Locke's role in legitimatizing the value of the African American experience, noted the following:

> He gave him [The New Negro] dreams to dream, but dreams that could be fulfilled, visions that could be attained; he gave him a sense of belonging, a cause to struggle for, more than anyone else, he contributed to removing from the Negro the stigma of inferiority and gave him social and human dignity as Emerson and Thoreau a century before gave it to the American [European Americans]. He gave the Negro a consciousness of being a part of mankind in general, a partner in man's creative progress. Many a Negro today walks with straighter gait, holding his [her] head high in any company, because of Alain Locke.[83]

Others who spoke compassionately at Locke's funeral described him as "generous," "patient," and "selfishless," having "uncommon compromising quality," and "breadth of knowledge," "universally respected," "courteous and courageous," and "perceptive and sensitive." Eugene Holmes, one of the many Locke protégés, provides a graphic description of Locke as a visionary:

> And Alain Locke, more prophetic and Cassandra-like than he could have ever known in the last article written before his death ["Minority Side of Intercultural Education," Education for Cultural Unity: Seventeenth Yearbook, California Elementary School Principals Association, n.d., 60-64] said, "it is to this mirror that I turn for the salient changes of majority attitude toward the Negro, and equally important, for a view of the Negro's changed attitude toward himself. For the Negro seems at last on the verge of proper recognition and a fraternal acceptance as a welcome participant and collaborator in the American Arts. Should this become the realized goal, the history of the Negro's strange and tortuous career in American literature may became also the story of America's hard-won but easily endured attainment of cultural democracy."[84]

Unfortunately, most Americans remain unaware of Locke's overall impact on the social history of this country, and how he specifically envisioned adult education as a conduit for achieving social and economic parity.

Two

ANDRAGOGY AND THE EDUCATION
OF AFRICAN AMERICAN ADULTS

> Let us, then, take the Negro case merely as a special instance of a general
> problem requiring special attention and effort, perhaps, because of its acute
> degree but in its significance and bearing on educational problems and
> methods considered generally diagnostic and universally applicable.
>
> Alain Leroy Locke[1]

The concept of andragogy presupposes a set of assumptions about how adults
learn, as opposed to pedagogy, which focuses on how youth learn. The
overarching principle is that learning for adults becomes a collaborative process, yet one that recognizes the importance of self-directedness in the instructional process. Critical to the formulation of an andragogical approach are methods and techniques for teaching. The andragogues would argue that techniques
and certainly material resources for learning must, of necessity, be different for
adults as opposed to children. In this context, Locke was truly an andragogue.
His discourse on the cultural approach to education as preferable to the conven-
tional-literacy approach to adult education, was indeed a recognition of the fact
that adults learn differently from children and thus require alternative instructional materials such as popular literature, audio and visual tools. In this respect, Locke stated, "the core of the problem of our field today is the development of the most effective techniques of mass education, bold and pioneering
experimentation with the new mass media of communication and enlightenment to make them serve constructively the social and cultural needs of even
larger segments of the people."[2] Furthermore, Locke emphasized the need for a
more uniquely conceived approach to teaching and learning for adults:

> We can too early make a fetish of literacy and [conformity] and deceive
> ourselves as to the scope and value of our gains. We can also waste too
> much effort, time, and money in what is after all a conventional pedagogic
> from the regular school curriculum.[3]

In his most recent work, *Applying Modern Principles of Adult Education*,
Malcolm Knowles considers Locke's early struggle to appropriately label the
new and evolving art and science of teaching adults. In the following scenario,

he provides a historical context for the appearance of the term "andragogy" in the literature of adult education:

> I found the solution in the summer of 1967, when a Yugoslavian adult educator, Dusan Savicevic, attended my summer session course on adult learning and at the end of it exclaimed, "Malcolm you are preaching and practicing andragogy." I responded, "Whatagogy?" because I had never heard the term before. He explained that European adult educators had coined the term as a parallel to pedagogy, to apply a label for the growing body of knowledge and technology in regard to adult learning, and that it was being defined as "the art and science of helping adults learn." It made sense to me to have a differentiating label, and I started using the term in 1968, in articles describing my theoretical framework for thinking about adult learning.[4]

Knowles posits two underlying assumptions that serve as a broad context for explicating andragogy.[5] They constitute: (1) a set of assumptions about adults as learners, and (2) a series of recommendations for the planning, management, and evaluation of adult learning. He emphasizes two major propositions: (1) intrinsic to adulthood is a sense of self-directedness; and (2) incongruous with this self-directedness, andragogical practice is a collaborative venture which involves the learner in most or all institutional functions. The issue of self-directedness is a rather "ticklish" one since Daniel Pratt observes that even for some adults, a function of self-directedness might involve relinquishing independent decision-making in deference to the authority of the institution. The implication is that andragogy should encompass and acknowledge both self-directedness and dependency.[6]

In a speech/paper, "What Adults Want to Learn," Locke outlined the need for adult education among African Americans. Three reasons were particularly noted: (1) education in youth was insufficient and sustaining for adulthood; (2) recurrent education was necessary in order to keep pace with changing world conditions; and (3) the demands of an ever-increasing technological society require adaptation of new strategies for living.[7] Essentially, the aforementioned reasons were a reinforcement and restatement of the observation made by John Hope and Mae Hawes that "adult education is necessary because the world is changing so rapidly that however well one may be educated, unless he keeps up and continues to make adjustments, he [she] finds himself [herself] behind the procession."[8] We need only consider the rapid escalation of computer technology and cybernetics in the 1990s that have continued into the twenty-first century. Recurrent education has significantly focused on the acquisition or honing of computer skills. Unfortunately, the jurors are out in terms of the long-term impact of the changing character of the workplace. For instance, interpersonal skills may very well be sacrificed at the expense of e-mails, and in Lockean terms, conjecturally could impact adversely on how individuals and groups relate to each other.

Locke places in a larger context the need for a transformation of purpose and mission in adult education by first noting:

> Adult education efforts today have no core program and little, if any, common denominator objectives. Can they and should they? That seems the critical question. Certainly no adequate answer can be expected from the present semi-vocational, semi-cultural or semi-recreational objectives which between them, seem to motivate so regrettably large amounts of adult education activity. Not that these are bad in themselves, but even they would function better as a marginal fringe to a more seriously conceived and professionally directed core program expressing a common consensus as to what in common the average adult needed in his continuing informal education.[9]

He continues with an assessment of prior efforts:

> Historically, two such generally accepted core objectives have galvanized and documented adult educative effort, the "illiteracy crusade" and the "Americanization program [designed for European immigrants, not formerly enslaved African Americans]. Unfortunately, both were at the subnormal level, but in spite of these limitations were constructively useful and gained wide public support and respect for adult education in general.[10]

He went on to suggest the nature of the core philosophy and curriculum for adult education, thus capturing the essence of his recommendations.

> My hunch as to the proper answer stems from the unprecedented reception, — the promotion of social maturity for all and at all levels, without regard to age, race, sex, class, formal training, and in a perspective of true democratic scope, that is to say, some tolerant and understanding citizenship of the community, the nation and the world. After all in this reorientation of values and attitude, it is the changed mind, the emancipated social attitudes which currently count.[11]

Then, Locke explores the challenge for professionals to formulate curricula that reflect a meaningful purpose, by noting:

> So that with a deliberate and enthusiastic consensus of opinion on this point of view and approach, all sorts and varieties of educative content could be focused, unified and cooperatively coordinated. The main core

content, however, would have to be worked out by competent professionals and in addition to giving more authority and coherence, this necessary
step would restore the central guidance of adult education where it properly belongs, to the field of the professional rather than the amateur educator.[12]

Nevertheless, Locke underscores the problems when he notes that "in the early
days, adult education for or by Negroes was conducted only by such organizations as the Church, the YMCA, the YWCA, parent-teacher associations, feder-
ated women's clubs, and the various branches of the National Urban League"
and observes that "there was little or no coordination and integration of programs." Ira Reid supports these claims and needs when he observed:

> In addition to these basic reasonings, it was stated that: First, there was a
> large group of illiterates among Negroes, which is a drag on the whole
> race. Second, that nearly three-fourths of all Negro children never get
> beyond the fourth grade. Third, the education which has been received
> has been below standard in terms of teacher preparation, equipment, cur-
> riculum, and administrative procedures. For this reason, it was felt that
> Negroes were in greater need of adult education of all kinds than perhaps
> any group in the United States.[13]

The aforementioned observations made by Reid over sixty years ago mirror
some of the criticisms of public education made by Jonathan Kozol in his 1995
publication, *Savage Inequalities*. Locke would be terribly demoralized by the
slow pace of change. As a matter of fact, he would have expected that at this
juncture in the social history of America, there would be no need to discuss the
woes of African American education in a vacuum, but that we should have
achieved an integrated society focused on the collective good. Locke's proposal is compelling when he notes, "Beyond the mere literacy level, enlarging
horizons and broadening human values must dominate it [adult education]."[14]
Simply put, Locke was perceptive in suggesting that the United States in terms
of social and economic stability should have a vested interest in adult education, particularly the education of African American adults.

The above comments have contemporary implications as many states,
including New York, grapple with changing demographics (significant increase
in black and hispanic populations) in relationship to potential work force needs
and the available pool of trained workers. Consequently, the role of adult education in its broader sense is as relevant in the 1990s as in the 1930s. The issue
of need and how to respond, continues to be a compelling issue.

The basic approach for teaching African American adults that was advocated by Locke embraced methodologies that infused cultural and historical
appreciation. However, the larger and more pointed question is centered on
how Locke incorporated dimensions of his philosophy of values generally, and

his philosophical perspectives on African American adult education, specifically, in the formulation of andragogical models.

As previously noted, Locke challenged the applicability of methods and techniques of conventional literacy teaching normally used with youth. This concern was addressed before numerous audiences. In a speech delivered at the annual meeting of the Adult Education Association in 1934, Locke took the organization to task for its adherence to and propagation of a "conventional pedagogic objective borrowed uncritically from the regular school curriculum." In that same presentation ("Trends in Adult Education for Negroes"), he suggested less authoritatively the following:

> I am not enough of a specialist to suggest in specific detail the best procedures and techniques, but I do throw forward the suggestion that visual and oral aids be effectively and decisively mobilized in our type of education and used with an eye to mass scale and effect. Certainly with regard to the Negro [African American] or any such disadvantaged group, of whom there are millions more than the illiterate and semi-illiterate Negroes, I can sense the futility of the homeopathic pill dosage that are too often an imitation of the elementary school procedure and materials inevitably involves. They [African American adults] must be deluged with enlightenment, though change is already seasoned and open, and made assimilable in terms of practical common sense and practical life situations.[15]

The above cited observation by Locke is reminiscent of the subsequent thinking and philosophy of Paulo Freire, who addresses the dichotomy of banking versus purposive education; the former suggesting that teachers feed information to students and they merely regurgitate the information, and the latter implying that they educate learners with a variety of thematic purposes in mind. Freire believed, as did Locke, that people must be educated not simply for "education's sake," but education must constitute a transforming catalyst for changing aspects of the human condition. Though their methods and approaches may have been different, both Freire and Locke viewed education as a catalyst for the social, political, and economic enlightenment of the adult masses.[16] The ultimate result as envisioned by both Locke and Freire would be the full participation of the masses in the social, political, and economic systems that impact on their lives. Social and cultural literacy played key roles in the readiness of the masses to empower themselves.

Consequently, Locke's educational philosophy was well reflected in his pleas to those assembled at the 1934 Adult Education Association meeting to acknowledge the needs of African Americans in education. However, he later cautions:

> Adult education particularly in this field of Negro [African American] need, is too orthodox in its techniques and too conservative in its objec-

tives. The general results even of widening effort and increasing public response are still too superficial for really vital and satisfactory results. A change of techniques and tactics is therefore rather imperative, whether that involves a shift from the main established agencies of service, in force at present or not, extension public school agencies and the public welfare educational services. Competing for the Negro mass audience for the moment come the relatively new agencies of the labor union and volunteer racial organizations, interested in mass education largely in its civic and cultural aspects.[17]

He continues with a critique of new and evolving programs:

These new programs are making considerable appeal although yet neither is well organized or planned. Their popularity arises mainly from their immediate touch with the practical problems of the man [or woman] in the street, and the morale technique which stimulates unequal zeal and interest on the part of even the most apathetic groups when once they become convinced of the lack of formality and condescension too characteristic in much of the older varieties of adult education.[18]

Thus, he recommended the following:

Instead of a narrow, specialized, scientific type of education, of which the dawn of the twentieth century offered us a mirage, there now stands out clearly before us the more distant, but more real prospect of an education broadly cultural, deeply humanistic, thoroughly socialized, justified now for the first time by practical reasons and democratic motives. Education of the cultural type has thus in our judgement been given a new lease of life; in fact, has become our lease on the life itself.[19]

For Locke, mass education "must have a dynamic and enthusiasm – compelling drive."[20]

Throughout his career, Locke strongly advocated a new pedagogy (andragogy) that focused on inculcating democratic values through intercultural education. He notes:

Fortunately for the still younger generation progressive education is making considerable effort and headway in seeing to it that they shall become socially literate and culturally and inter-culturally mature. Adult education must, both for effective democracy and international peace, take up this uncompleted tasks.[21]

In his "More than Blasting Brick and Mortar," Locke asserts:

> It's not enough to raze ghettos. We must throw open men's [and women's] minds. Democracy is a living language of social behavior. The charge of American education is to teach it.[22]

Locke was quite innovative in his general approach to methods and materials for teaching adults, especially African American adults, and countered potential criticism about the use of visual aids and other innovative techniques. The following is excerpted from his "Trends in Adult Education for Negroes":

> This plea for education through visual channels, demonstrations and group activity programs does not minimize the medium of the book and pamphlet in adult education. Particularly for the Negro masses the inaccessibility of the printed materials, especially modern and progressive materials, is pathetic and alarming. Even communities with reasonably extensive adult education work have such poor library facilities that the sparks of literacy kindled may be expected to die out for want of intellectual fuel. The cheap and adequately illustrated pamphlet, the circulating and mobile library are the only modern solution of this problem, without, much effort in formal instruction may just as well be written off as wasted.[23]

Locke was a visionary in terms of emphasizing the need for new and innovative technologies and methods for educating adults. Interestingly, current and continuing developments in the design of innovative systems for delivery of educational services have been greatly enhanced by telecommunications, computer hardware and software satellite dishes, and a variety of educational delivery systems that extend the realm of teaching and learning.

Locke further warned in "Negro Needs as Adult Education Opportunity":

> As a mere extension of traditional methods and values it [adult education] ceases to be worthy of its name; which is my reason for a final warning that adult education for Negroes [African Americans], or for that matter any group, cannot possibly be second-hand, traditional or conservatively directed. To the extent that we can influence it, we must see that it becomes increasingly progressive and experimental. If it is to serve minority group interest, this becomes more than desirable; it becomes imperative.[24]

The critical role of popularized literature as an organ for educating the masses, both European and African American, was strongly advocated by Locke and shared by others, including James Atkins, Special Assistant for Negro Affairs in the Office of Education at the time of the Second Annual Conference on

Adult Education and the Negro held at Tuskegee Institute, 1940. Atkins challenged adult education teachers, both white and African American, to teach
African American adults how to make use of the "vital stuff of Negro Life."[25] At
the same conference, Locke suggested that popularized literature serve "to better inform the white constituency with respect to the Negro and maybe even
more important to have the Negro constituents well informed about themselves."[26] The importance of information dissemination was underscored at the
Third Annual conference on Adult Education and the Negro, held at Howard
University, 1941. Locke was re-elected President of the Annual Conference. In
a press release regarding the conference, written by Otto McClarrin, Press Service, Howard University, the following is noteworthy:

> Adult education in the current American crisis was seen as necessary to
> help the Negro masses to maintain morale and understand the workings
> of a democracy. Adult Education will play an important role in assisting
> the Negro in discriminating between propaganda, truth and subversive
> information and influences. A program of information for the average
> Negro and arranged to meet and serve his wants, was seen as a major need
> in the current crisis. Community organizations to provide informational
> services to Negro groups was encouraged.[27]

As an andragogue, more in practice than in name, Locke's early ideals on
the appropriate approach to teaching adults in an atmosphere of mass education
bordered on an equalitarian and strongly African-centered philosophical perspective. For instance, he advocated in a rather idealistic manner, the democra-
tization of adult education, implying equal opportunity of access to the same
services; nevertheless, he acknowledged that the needs of African American
adult learners were different.

Locke, who as a philosopher objected to absolutism, and thus, was critical of
parochialism in adult education, was often torn between his philosophical perspectives and the realistic practice of adult education. In fact, Locke may have
experienced a series of conflicts in this regard. Absolutism posed a series of problems for Locke, who was concerned with the diabolical social predicaments of
African Americans and the resulting insidiousness of their plight in American society. Therefore, in terms of adult education, he argued that though the goals should
be the same for all groups, the experiences of African Americans required alternative approaches and strategies. Consequently, for Locke, as David Joseph Burgett
observes, "social and cultural reciprocity, on an equal basis, among cultures of
varying ideologies, all existing within an essentially monistic framework is a contradiction."[28] Absolutism was anathema to Locke's vision of a world that respected
and tolerated the plethora of diverse cultural entities and perspectives – a community that would value the imperatives of different groups. Also, though he agreed

that adult education should be the same for all, he argued for programs that acknowledged differences, thus, advocating a "special needs" approach to adult education, for instance, for African Americans.

Though Locke advocated strongly for what might be prospectively viewed as an African-centered approach to African American adult education, in some respects he might have been perceived as an accommodationist and cultural assimilationist. In his paper, "Areas of Extension," he separates the immediate need from the long-term goal:

> Whatever warrantable special emphases there may be can be justified only as special remedial and corrective procedures to overcome particular results of neglect, isolation or disparagement, and they may be regarded as temporary and transitional until the minority situation is brought up to educational par and put into a democratically integrated alignment. Ultimately, if we envisage a democratic national situation at all, we must hope to see all such special and separate programs absorbed as speedily as possible into general programs of mass education, such as community projects, worker's education, basic programs of publicly supported adult education.[29]

Locke is saying that until parity occurs in education, a state that can be achieved only through cultural remediation, there will be no realization of educational democracy. Thus, tension arises between Locke's assimilationist posture, his objection to the notion of a "melting pot," and his optimism about the integration of race-based programs into the larger mosaic of adult education programs. I would argue that Locke may have been strategically assimilationist in his short-term policies because he was striving for the ultimate goal of even-handed cultural acceptance of difference.

The reader should bear in mind that Locke's frame of reference in a larger context was the ultimate realization of a culturally pluralist, global society, in which differences become *non sine gravitas*. The short-term goals to be reached are, for example, remediation and parity.

In his presentation at the first National Conference on Adult Education and the Negro, held at Hampton Institute, Hampton, Virginia, 21-22 October 1938, under the auspices of the American Association for Adult Education, the Associates in Negro Folk Education, and the Extension Department of Hampton Institute, Locke passionately declared:

> Let us, then, take the Negro [African American] case merely as a special instance of a general problem, requiring special attention and effort perhaps because of its acute degree, but in its significance and bearing upon educational problems and methods considered generally diagnostic and universally applicable. The condition of the Negro and its educational implications will fit and parallel any similar circumstanced group, and in addition, like many another acute situation, will point the lesson of new and generally applicable techniques.[30]

As he consistently advocated for mass social education, Locke concurrently challenged the legitimacy and viability of "rugged individualization," ingrained in the American ethos. He asserts that:

> We Americans, traditional individualists that we are, do not seem to like either the term or the idea of mass education, believing — erroneously I think — that the educating of individuals cumulatively adds up to the same thing and automatically leads to mass rationality and social enlightenment. But call it what you will, mass education or folk education — I confess to liking the latter term — we cannot be at odds over the eventual, commonly accepted objectives of adult education. This is a democratic widening of all sorts of educative opportunities and experiences for more and more people over greater areas not only of knowledge and understanding.[31]

Locke emphasized the critical importance of relevant cultural and historical materials for teaching African Americans. He further admonishes:

> Adult education seems to me to misdirect its own deepest aims in not immediately embarking on a strenuous program of health, civic and social education at least as an auxiliary approach, and perhaps as a main approach. What is crucially important is an awakened, galvanized individual in place of the stagnant, conservative person who is the crude toddler of our process.[32]

The above observation by Locke is somewhat reminiscent of Freire's call for a kind of praxis that would transform the "culture of silence" to an energized mass movement directed at purposeful change.

The ideal of absolutism and the imposition of "standards" are social bedfellows. Locke would argue that standards are necessary to maintain some degree of balance, order, and sanity in a democracy. On the other hand, Locke would strongly object to ill-conceived standards that are arbitrarily and capriciously applied, and that serve only to subjugate, oppress, and inflict psychological damage on the powerless in society. To suggest that only one standard way of doing or thinking exists would be appalling and absurd to Locke. A case in point is the contemporary controversy over I.Q. as a standardized measure of intelligence. New research argues that the traditional understanding of intelligence is grounded in absolutism, whereas in fact a more relativistic perspective reveals the existence of not one but "multiple intelligences."[33] Thus, the manner and ways in which individuals and groups negotiate what Johnny Washington calls "destinicity" may be quite fluid and varied rather than conditional on absolutism, which has no place in adult education, if for no other reason than the realization that the life experiences of individuals and groups vary.[34]

Three

CONTRIBUTIONS TO THE ADULT
EDUCATION MOVEMENT

Locke's contributions to the adult education movement might seem paradoxical to some observers. Here was an erudite African American scholar of philosophy who emerged as one of the central leaders of the Harlem Renaissance. Consequently, it seems reasonable to question his embrace of what on the surface appears far removed from his professional, intellectual, artistic, and cultural interests. Therefore, several observations might serve to bridge the gap. First, one might ask why a philosopher, and black philosopher at that, would take an active interest in adult education. Since adult education as an evolving process relied significantly on the insights of scholars across such disciplines as sociology, psychology, and history, inclusion of a philosopher with impeccable credentials, who could provide yet another perspective culled from a different discipline, was important for the reputation of an area of critical inquiry that lacked a defined epistemology and coherent purpose. Thus, Locke was recruited by the movement, saw the need, and responded to it.

Second, Locke's race was a plus for the movement, which recognized the need for inclusiveness. Yet, little did the leadership expect that Locke would not be content with assuming the role of "the spook who sat by the door." To the contrary, he personified an instrument for radical change in both transforming the philosophy and direction of adult education in America.

Again, what is particularly revealing is the observation that Locke did not consciously gravitate to the movement. As Gyant states:

> Although his interest in adult education started in 1918, it was not until 1924 that Locke became active in the adult education movement. It was at this time that F. P. Keppel, President of the Carnegie Foundation, asked him to serve as delegate to the first conference on adult education.[1]

However, in retrospect, it appears that Locke had already cultivated a series of relationships with known figures and organizations associated with adult education. Holmes, for instance, observes:

> His [Locke's] connections were also with the Kellogs who edited THE SURVEY AND SURVEY GRAPHICS, The Harmon Foundation, The Rosenwald Foundation, The General Education Association, The Forum on the Air, The American Library Association and many others.[2]

So, Locke's involvement in adult education was a natural evolution.

Several additional observations should be considered in chronicling Locke's contributions to the adult education movement generally and his leadership, tenacity, and insistence on the inclusion of African Americans in the "master plan" for an adult education revolution in the United States. First, as a "token" in a white dominated organization, The American Association for Adult Education, Locke was to symbolize the consciousness of the inner sanctum of the leadership in confronting the exclusion of African Americans in both leadership and programmatic efforts. The plight of African Americans in this country symbolized for Locke a failure of democracy, and for him, adult education could be instrumental in righting the historical "wrong." Therefore, basic literacy was appropriate, yet adult education could serve other needs. For instance, he opined: "Social education is [essential] for democratic living, for squaring democratic practice with democratic theory and values."[3]

Locke implored the leaders and practitioners in the field to coalesce around what was evolving as not simply an educational movement, but a social movement that had the potential to impact significantly on the course of race relations and economic and political equality in America. His call for a common ground among adult educationists is captured in the following:

> [It] will become a crusade, enlisting the common loyalty and effort of all of us, or certainly all intelligent enough to realize the significance of the situation and its critical demands.[4]

Second, it is not hyperbole to suggest that Locke's engaging presence in the American Association for Adult Education served as an effective catalyst in attracting and galvanizing other African American educators, professionals, and grassroots workers to the movement.

As *cause célèbre*, Locke, through his leadership in the adult education movement generally, and his tenacity in bringing public attention to the needs of African American adult learners, specifically, left an indelible stamp on the transformation of adult education. The depth of his commitment to change is embodied by three outstanding programs. They are the pioneering experiments in adult education for African Americans, conducted in Harlem and Atlanta during the period 1931–1934; the publication of a series of study materials called Bronze Booklets, designed to inform readers about the history and culture of African Americans; and the convening of three unprecedented national conferences that focused on the educational needs of African American adults. Certainly not to be discounted is his emergence as President of the American Association for Adult Education in 1946. Let us take a look at his sterling accomplishments, which follow.

1. The Harlem and Atlanta Experiments

The Harlem and Atlanta Experiments in Negro Adult Education, as they were called, were sponsored by the American Association for Adult Education with financial support from the Carnegie Corporation and the Julius Rosenwald Fund. Days notes that "Alain Locke served the two experiments as a consultant and evaluator."[5] The Harlem and Atlanta projects were based at local library sites, the 135th Street library of the New York Public Library and the Auburn Avenue branch of the Carnegie Library in Atlanta. Reid contrasts the atmosphere at each site when noting that the program at the Harlem site would likely be enhanced by the existence of the internationally known Schomburg Center of Negro Life and History (later changed to the Schomburg Center for Research in Black Culture).[6] Sinnette observes that Arthur Schomburg was "a leading member of the community advisory committee" and played a critical role in the project, which recognized the collection under his curatorship as the "backbone of the experiment."[7] Conversely, Reid reports that the challenge to the Atlanta experiment lay in the fact that the branch setting had little community support and lacked a working relationship with community agencies.[8]

The opportunity for both programs to effectively impact the African American community was nevertheless high. The objectives were broad and allowed for creative program development. Reid, in drawing from the evaluation report submitted by Ernestine Rose, director of the Harlem experiment, summarizes:

Its original purpose was to outline and conduct an informal program embracing the economic, social and cultural phases of adult education. It was conditioned by two factors; namely, that it must be of a type adaptable to the purposes and program of a library, and, that it was promoted and its policies directed and developed, not by the librarian alone, but by a committee of community leaders acting in an advisory capacity to the librarian-executive.[9]

Each program had its distinct programmatic character. Harvey G. Neufeldt and Leo McGee offer the following description of the Harlem program:

The Harlem experiment operated out of the 135th Street branch of the New York Public Library, later the Schomburg Center for Research in Black Culture, and sought to expand the cultural, vocational, and social horizons of Black residents in Harlem. Discussion groups on contemporary literature, drama, modern social thought, art appreciation, and lecture courses on parent education, Black history, and adult efficiency were offered.[10]

In a subsequent report on the Harlem experiment to Morse Cartwright, executive director of the American Association of Adult Education, Ernestine Rose reported that the program had been expanded to include a "Readers Advisory Service."[11] According to Rose, "this service is designed to cooperate with the adult education program in all its projects, short lists of reading being made available in each subject treated." Her report indicates that the activities of the library-centered programs were very diverse. They included, but were not limited to, visual arts, choral singing, history lectures (ingratiated by the Schomburg Collection), book talks, parent education classes, and counseling and social work services.

The Harlem Experiment was not without its controversies. For instance, Sinnette observes that Franklin Hopper, a consultant to the Advisory Committee, expressed concern about deleterious and various antagonistic factions in the community, believing that Arthur Schomburg had "the universal respect of all factions and behind the scenes, was able to smooth out many situations to hold the group together."[12] However, Sinnette also cites a letter of Schomburg to fellow bibliophile, Wendell Dabney, in which Schomburg questioned Locke's ability to relate to the black masses for whom the program was intended, for Schomburg found Locke to be "too pedantic and lacking the easy manner essential for dealing with ordinary Harlemites."

Throughout the three-year period of the experiment, some practitioners in the field remained critical of certain aspects of the Harlem project. Sara E. Reid, Field Project Secretary, cited the problem of the increasing number of programs that either overlapped or were duplications of existing programs.[13] Ira Reid found a lack of diversity in constituencies served (for example, too many drawn by the emotional appeal of some groups, including, Father Divine followers and so-called Negro Intelligentsia), and an insufficient number of adult education teachers.[14] Yet, in spite of potential obstacles to program success, the noteworthy Harlem program made obvious gains and garnered substantial praise. For instance, Morgan states that the program "enabled the library (135th Street branch) to regain its former prominence in adult education."[15] According to Ernestine Rose, the Harlem program created an awareness in the Harlem community of the general need for adult education, and the pivotal role of the library in responding to the specific interests of African American adult learner.[16]

This assessment was corroborated by Days, who observed that "the public library emerged from the experiment as a powerful and effective agency in the delivery of adult education services within the community."[17] Particularly noteworthy is the program's emphasis on responding to the needs of constituents being served, allowing for program flexibility. Ernestine Rose states, "thus far the work has been largely experimental in character. Where interest failed or the methods used proved unwise, the experiment has been altered or abandoned. Where there has been response and where the need is evident, there effort has been concentrated. The keenest interest has been shown in the fields of economic thought, social education, artistic expression, and Negro solidarity."

Though the Atlanta Experiment was demographically similar to the Harlem project in terms of the concentration of African Americans, it was shaped by two factors: the homogeneity of its African American community; and the pressure of existing social institutions, such as the church. Days notes that "because the influence of the churches is probably broader than any other agency, the director began by interviewing the ministers."[18] In her first year's report, Mae Hawes, Project Director, recorded:

> Letters were sent out to fifty outstanding ministers asking for a personal conference. At least 50 percent, responded. In some instances, the conferences were lengthy but were revealing. This time was well spent, as it seems to us.[19]

The approach in Atlanta was more "top-down" than "bottom-up," as in the New York City experiment. There was indeed a systematic and methodical effort to communicate with existing agencies and organizations to assess local program needs. The ultimate thrust in the Atlanta experiment was how best to coordinate existing services and to provide support. But the Harlem experiment focused on creating new programs in response to constituency needs. Days provides a description offered by the Atlanta Program:

> The programs offered by the Atlanta project were Readers Advisory Service, which is the mainstay of public libraries, generally; compilation of subject bibliographies; and working with established groups such as Parent-Teacher Associations and Federated Women's Clubs. From the beginning in 1931 until 1934, the Atlanta experiment reported organizing and sponsoring the following groups — 103 church women studying modern problems as they concern women; 200 public school and college teachers studying international educational and social problems; ministers groups studying economics; family relations groups, and citizenship groups in cooperation with the League for Industrial Democracy; cooperation with night schools to combat illiteracy through the creation of suitable elementary instructional materials for adults and assisting literary clubs by giving program suggestions and by supplying books and other materials from the library collection.[20]

As with the Harlem experiment, some adult educators were highly critical of the Atlanta project. Eliza Gleason commented that "the Atlanta experiment was handicapped by its conforming to the standards and programs of the Negro branch of the Carnegie Library in Atlanta."[21] These sentiments were shared by Ira Reid.[22] Continuing her critique of the Atlanta project, Gleason reported the following:

Though the majority of Negro branch libraries are ill-equipped to cope satisfactorily with problems of a progressive adult education program, there is need for a greater sensitivity to the potential contribution which the public library can make in the field of adult education.[23]

Some criticism appeared along gender lines. Sara E. Reid reverberates the observation of Mae Hawes, Director of the Atlanta Project, that the "program as it developed in Atlanta appealed more to men than it did to women."[24] Ira Reid criticized the limited participation of black churches as significant in limiting program success. He states, "The church is by far the foremost social institution among Negroes. It did not participate to any great extent in the Atlanta experiment."[25]

Nevertheless, the Atlanta experimental program attracted both national and international interest. The president of Tennessee Agricultural and Industrial State College, for instance, expressed an interest in the Atlanta Experiment in relationship to the proposed expansion program.[26] Also, a request came in from Burean Manuel Training and Industrial School in Philadelphia.[27] Other requests came from students working on Masters theses.[28] The World Association for Adult Education (London) requested information on the program "in order that we may be in a position to make it known in other parts of the world."[29]

Mae Hawes was confident about the overall impact of the program:

It is evident that this project will make a definite contribution to the educational world in Atlanta; that the attitudes and philosophies of a large percent of the Negro population will be changed and reconditioned and that the objective — continuous growth of personality by training his judgment, by adding to his knowledge and by increasing his wisdom will grow into ever widening circles.[30]

The experimental program in both Harlem and Atlanta spanned almost three years, in spite of some initial objection from the Executive Director of the American Association for Adult Education, Morse Cartwright, who was opposed to the race consciousness aspect of the programs. Morgan observes, "Cartwright was personally against social action and he counseled that education should follow rather than lead the trends of the times."[31]

Yet, at the completion of the program period, for various phases of annual project activities, even some antagonists were converted. Cartwright, noted the following in an "Annual Report from the Director" following the first year of the experiment:

The Association's two adult education programs for Negroes, initiated on an experimental basis in 1931–1932 in Atlanta and in the Harlem district of New York, have flourished through the year and have presented proof of the sympathetic attitude toward education on the part of adult Negroes, both in a northern and southern city. The committee in charge of the two projects are most enthusiastic and each has formulated extensive plans for the further conduct of the experiment.[32]

Arthur Schomburg, as Sinnette intimates, "was decidedly more pessimistic about the eventual outcome" of the program in Harlem.[33] Yet, in a rather informal assessment of the program, Schomburg[34] suggests that "the Harlem experiment was especially innovative in the character and breadth of its activities."[34]

Locke was tapped by the American Association for Adult Education to evaluate the experimental projects. Morse Cartwright, Executive Director, in his "Annual Report of the Director," announced Locke's selection and lauded his qualification to assume the task. The following was culled from his report:

> An allocation of $1,000 from the adult education experimental fund, made by the Carnegie Corporation upon recommendation of the Association, has made it possible to secure the services of Alain Locke, Professor of Philosophy at Howard University, as observer and appraiser of the two enterprises. Locke will make frequent visits to New York and Atlanta from his home in Washington, D.C.; will advise with the committee in charge in the two cities, and at the close of the third year of the experiments, that is at the end of 1933–1934, will file with the Association a report on the accomplishments of the two experiments. It is obviously of great advantage to the Association to assure an outside point of view from a Negro Educator of high standing. Locke is in full sympathy with the objectives of the experiments and is interested also in the Association's desire to check the results in a northern city against the results in a southern city.[35]

Though I would not question Locke's competency to effectively and efficiently facilitate the program evaluation, it is possible that his closeness to the Harlem Experiment contaminated his ultimate report on that project.

Beyond the important question of Locke's qualifications to evaluate the programs is also the recognition by the American Association for Adult Education of the profound need for such programs. As previously cited, Sara E. Reid provides the rationale that supported the association's decision to establish the two experimental programs.[36]

The resulting fourteen-page report was entitled "Report on Negro Adult Education Projects," dated 15 March 1934.[37] This report had been preceded by a letter to Morse Cartwright, Executive Director of the AAAE, in which Locke provided some preliminary findings, which included: (1) evidence of demonstrated need; and (2) need for greater coordination of existing organized institutional efforts in the area of adult education for African Americans.[38]

In the final report, Locke proceeded with a discussion of the strengths and weaknesses of each program; subsequently providing some general conclusions.

In discussing the Atlanta Project, Locke noted "the limited staff" and "meager resources" as primary program weaknesses.[39] However, he identified five positive results: (1) the need was "vindicated"; (2) the experiment demonstrated "sustained interest and enthusiasm of an interracial group of leading educators, librarians and prominent citizens"; (3) the program prompted "the complete reorganization and rehabilitation of the Auburn Street branch public library, underscoring the need for the extension of branch library facilities for the Negro population"; (4) through the participation of Atlanta and Emory universities, the educated class was put in contact with the masses, and "the teaching of social science to some students by practical activity rather than by preachment and exhortation"; and (5) a "broad range of interests [was] identified."[40] Locke found the most successful dimensions of the Atlanta program to be areas dealing with citizenship problems, household budgeting, and a book and photograph mobile service.

Locke's overall program assessment is captured in the following statement:

> With the net results as positive and constructive as they undoubtedly are, it is only fair to state that in my judgement the minor shortcomings of the Atlanta project to date have been delay, diffuseness and discontinuity. The first was obviously due mainly to the cautiousness of the approach with a new thing in a conservative community, — although the director should have had earlier staff assistance and more prompt provision of supplementary reading materials for the discussion groups. Having to rely on casual and haphazard cooperation of organizations and volunteer workers primarily accounts for the remaining defects; although more experience with adult education approaches and techniques would have corrected some of the disjointed tendencies in the program. Corrective concentration toward this end has already been recommended personally to the Director, and some program reconstructions made in accordance.[41]

In the section of the evaluation focusing on the Harlem Experiment, Locke initially commented that "the Harlem Project began with a very favorable start of some years of extension work by the 135th Street branch library along informal adult education lines."[42] The report identified three basic weaknesses: (1) the poor condition of the site; (2) overcrowding of activities, and (3) scheduling conflicts.

The programs considered most successful in the Harlem Project were (1) Summer Art workshop; (2) the Discussion Forum, which focused on a variety of economic, political issues; (3) Community Courses; (4) courses and lectures in Negro History greatly influenced by the existence of the Schomburg Collection and according to Locke, "the tireless services of Mr. Schomburg as guide and lecturer;" and (5) outdoor forum and park lectures and demonstrations in child welfare care.[43] Locke recommended that vocationally related courses not be taught in the library because other agencies were offering such opportunities for residents of the community. On the other hand, he recommended that "the success of the work in Negro History and in the Art Workshop are worthy of being reduced to a model syllabus outline and being publicized for the guidance of adult education groups elsewhere."[44] On this point, the subsequent evolution of the Bronze Booklet Series, to be discussed in the next section, becomes significant and pertinent.

In his assessment of the general and special areas of interest, Locke observed:

> In the Harlem experiment it was decided not to prejudge the situation but to include in the first offerings every possible variety of subject and approach. In retrospect, the general topics were hailed enthusiastically, but when the program was in operation the general interest activities fell off, while the response to subjects with racial appeal developed steadily momentum. The conclusion that the racial interest approach is more effective provide some important implications; it confirms our belief, derived from previous experience, that the adult must be met on the plane of living interests, even if they are parochial and one-sided, and from these as a starting point must be gradually led out into broader and deeper interests.[45]

Locke's charge was to evaluate two projects with an underlying assumption that contrasting needs would be the case. Yet, he cites in his report:

> The comparative results of the Harlem and the Atlanta experience do not indicate the anticipated differences between the needs and responses of Northern and Southern, metropolitan and small city types of community. With few exceptions, the trends of the results in the two centers have been similar, and have confirmed each other. Especially is this so with regard to the efficacy of the racial interest approach and appeal as the preferred element in the program.[46]

In discussing his "General Conclusions," Locke addressed the issue of race consciousness explicitly:

> While racial interests and problems have been found to be the items on these programs receiving the most enthusiastic and sustained response, and are thus to be recommended as the most effective motivation for programs of adult study in Negro communities, both programs at Harlem and Atlanta have wisely incorporated a considerable, in fact large number of general items and subjects. The experience suggests no arbitrary curtailment of a normal program, but merely the pivoting of a reasonable proportion of the work around the racial interest and appeal. It is amazing to

discover how seldom those natural and inevitable interests are catered to for Negro adults upon the intellectual and informational plane; since the general tone of the press, pulpit and informal discussion is yet so lamentably emotional and propagandist.[47]

He continues:

The outstanding result of the experiences in these projects in my judgement has been the demonstration of an eager and appreciative response to racial information and discussion of an intellectual, informative and non-propagandist character. Evidently here is a medium of major importance and effect for correcting the warped bias and relieving the morbid tension handicap and social injustice have inflicted on the average Negro mind and spirit. In this connection, too, it is important to note the considerable amount of inter-racial interest and contact evoked, even in a reactionary southern community, by the racial features of such a program such as Negro music, drama and art, and the intelligent, objective discussion of racial problems and relations.[48]

Locke subsequently underscored the critical role of race-based curriculum and programs as critical to the success of adult education initiatives directed at African Americans. He notes:

The task of adult educationists . . . lies in discovering and using ways to generate serious and sustained interests. For the Negro, the one word "race," with all its mental association, is a tragically magic charm that instantly evokes dead serious thought. Provided we do not overwork the appeal of this charm, this special interest of the Negro. I believe that we have in it a positive focusing point for mass adult education.[49]

Ira Reid, social scientist at Atlanta University, made poignant observations regarding future implications of the experimental projects. The following comments are noteworthy:

1. Few of the agencies conducting any adult education work among Negroes have any broad or accurate concept of the adult education movement and its objectives.
2. As in all phases of informal adult education among all groups, there is a need for developing adequate leadership and a danger in utilizing those willing to volunteer who are usually ill-equipped to inspire, who have utmost faith in the finality of their opinions, who may be good teachers of facts but failures at presenting the education that culturally enlarges life.

3. The necessity of increasing the Negro's appreciation of the library and adapting the library to his needs in reading and the development of reading habits.

4. The necessity of correlated programs in adult education so that programs are considered rather than agencies.

5. The possibilities of a racial program that avoids chauvinism and propaganda.

6. The place of art and song in a program with Negro adults that may be centered around folk art and folk music.

7. That the Negro's interests are equally as keen in social and economic questions as other individuals today; and that they are often colored by a racial interest which must be intelligently but objectively considered.

8. Neither experiment touched in deep numbers either the professional and "intellectual" group or real masses. People affected were in between these two — those who might have been interested even prior to the program. Is the library the wrong place to begin with the masses? Must the "intellectuals" remain a self-sufficient and isolated group?

9. Last and most important of lessons, — a lack of coordination and its critical importance in building a successful adult education program.[50]

Although those associated with and actively engaged in the projects came to a general consensus regarding the success of the programs, the funding sources were reluctant to continue supporting the programs beyond the three-year exerimental period. A letter from the Rosenwald Fund to Morse Cartwright, Executive Director of AAAE bears out this latter observation. It states:

> Over $700,000 was spent on library extension projects [including Harlem and Atlanta Projects]. Also, we believe that library branches are able to carry themselves fairly well from now on there is nothing very distinctive that would be added by further aid from us.[51]

Regrettably, within the ranks of the American Association for Adult Education, no outpouring of support occurred for the continuation and expansion of the projects *vis-a-vis* additional funding. For instance, a letter from Eugene Kinckle Jones, Adviser on Negro Affairs for the Development of Education and a member of the Harlem Project advisory committee to Morse Cartwright, is revealing:

> I acknowledge receipt of your letter of May 14th, advising me as to the attitude of members of your Executive Committee concerning the field service activity proposed in our plan for the Adult Education Services to Negroes. Under normal conditions I would accept this as final without

comment as there would be no reason for abandoning the policy of the Association in approaching the subject among Negroes, but in view of the fact that we have not developed National Negro Professional leadership in the Adult Education field in keeping with our hopes of three years ago, it would seem to me that the time is now ripe for us to subsidize some person who can develop along this line. It was not my thought nor do I think it was Locke's that we would have some central point from which stimulation, encouragement, and promotion of the adult education idea would be promulgated among Negroes in various communities throughout the country. In other words, our idea was that Mr. Ira Reid (representing both type and scholastic ability) would be the person to have the relationship to the colored movement similar to which you have for the movement at large.[52]

Jones concludes his letter by advocating for the continuing funding of the Harlem and Atlanta projects. Given the tone of the exchanged letters, the funding sources and the AAAE leadership feared the loss of control over programs that would be directed at the African American community. On one hand, one of the underlying objectives of the experimental projects was to develop a cadre of African American leaders in the field. On the other hand, a growing fear was that any such emerging leadership in the African American community would pose a power threat to the larger white community. The potential for unleashing power through literacy may have indeed bred contempt.

Unfortunately, the end result was the discontinuation of subsidies for the projects originally funded by the Carnegie Corporation and the Rosenwald Fund. Yet, in spite of the imminent demise of the projects, the following laudatory comments by Days represents a testament to Locke's emergence as a leader in the field:

Perhaps the major consequence of the projects was that Alain Leroy Locke emerged as a leading champion of adult education for Black Americans. He became considered by the AAAE and similar organizations as the one person to consult in assessing the needs of Blacks when designing adult education experiences.[53]

The leadership of the Harlem and Atlanta communities deserve credit for their tenacity and ultimate decision to forge ahead. Consequently, the decision of the funding sources did not cause a total dismantling of the adult education programs in Harlem and Atlanta. In Harlem, many of the programs were maintained and/or expanded under the auspices of the City Department of Adult Education in cooperation with such groups as the New York Urban League, the Abyssinian Church, the Y.W.C.A., and the Y.M.C.A. In Atlanta, a number of the organizations and committees that emerged during the tenure of the adult education experiment continued to function on some level. The Atlanta Association for the Study of Educational Problems, which had garnered a respectable level of visibility and reputation in the Atlanta area.[54] Using the community lecture mode, this organization whose membership included John Hope, then President of Atlanta University, created a forum for the discussion of a broad range of educational issues, with local, national, as well as international import. The topics ranged from "Trends in Modern Education" to "Education in Russia."

Locke was not to be dissuaded nor demoralized by the lack of support for the continuation of the Harlem and Atlanta programs. He moved expeditiously to organize Associates in Negro Folk Education. The aim of this organization was to disseminate facts and information about the history and culture of African Americans in a manner that would be comprehensible to the masses of people. The vehicle was the publication of a series of Bronze Booklets. A letter from Morse Cartwright to Locke gives approval for the project.[55]

2. Associates in Negro Folk Education

Locke was tireless in his efforts to extend in some newly developed venue the work of the Harlem and Atlanta projects. Consequently, the creation of the Associates in Negro Folk Education was to symbolize and eventually actualize this aim. The underlying objective was to teach the culture and history of African Americans to an African American mass audience. Thus, Locke envisioned an association that would disseminate accurate and substantive information about the African American experience. His firm belief was that if African Americans were to successfully impact on the larger American culture and society, it was imperative that the community achieve a sense of collective identity, and thus, a knowledge and understanding of its contributions to the larger global community.

Locke perceived the Bronze Booklets as a strategy for garnering additional support for more adult education initiatives for African Americans, as well as portentously influencing broader policy issues. The study materials that were to emerge, which included African American art, music and drama, were also aimed at providing legitimacy to the historical and cultural richness of the African American presence in the United States.

As Sinnette informs us, "the adult community education projects for blacks in New York City and Atlanta, Georgia, led to the formation of the Associates in Negro Folk Education."[56] Locke was the founder and chair, and Arthur Schomburg was a founding member, along with Charles S. Johnson, Eugene Kinckle Jones, Mary McLeod Bethune, Franklin Hopper, and Lyman Bryson.

The mission of the organization is elucidated on the last page of each of its Bronze Booklet Series. It reads as follows:

> This project has grown out of certain stimulating experiments in adult education conducted for the last four years in Harlem and Atlanta by local

committees, sponsored by the Rosenwald Fund and the Carnegie Corporation of New York.[57]

In a speech delivered at the fourteenth Annual Meeting of the American Association for Adult Education, held in Ontario, Canada, in June 1940, Locke provides a rationale for the need to publish the Bronze Booklets. The theme of the
conference was "Minorities and Democracy: An Opportunity for American Adult
Education." In his talk, Locke unapologetically articulates, in no uncertain terms,
the value of race-based education. The following is particularly poignant:

> The task of adult educationists, as I see it, lies in discovering and using ways
> to generate serious and sustained interests. For the Negro, the one word "race,"
> with all its mental associations, is a tragically magic charm that instantly
> evokes dead serious thought. Provided that we do not overwook the appeal
> of this charm, this special interest of the Negro, I believe that we have in it a
> positive focusing point for mass adult education.[58]

Envisioning the publication of the Bronze Booklets as one means of assessing
the value of race consciousness in forging a viable program of adult education,
Locke continued:

> This belief is soon to be tested through the publication and circulation of
> nine adult education booklets for Negroes, which are now in preparation
> under the auspices of a committee incorporated as "The Associates in Ne-
> gro Folk Education." The actual circulation of these booklets will not tell
> the story; rather the real criteria of the worth of the approach through ra-
> cial interest will be first, whether emotional spot interest can be raised to a
> sustained interest and, second, whether a special interest can develop into
> a vital general interest in the problems of contemporary life.[59]

For Locke, if race-based approaches were intellectually and socially engaging,
so be it. He concludes:

> I myself, am convinced that the key to an intellectual interest is a strong
> emotional drive and that Negro adult education should boldly capitalize
> the motivation of the racial interest and let the bogey of propaganda be
> hanged, if by this means we get desirable results of serious sustained inter-
> est and effort. For I believe that if sufficient air and ventilation are applied,
> out of red flame of propaganda we can generate the white light of social
> intelligence.[60]

Locke's optimism and agenda are revealed in the following statement:

Another grant from the Carnegie Corporation through the American Association for Adult Education would make possible the publication of special materials for the use of Negro adult education groups. These would consist of a series of syllabi in booklet form to be published in 1936 by the Associates in Negro Folk Education, a committee organized to promote adult education among Negro groups.[61]

The organization stated that because "progressive thinking on the questions of Negro life will best be stimulated by frank discussion and subjective opinion rather than by over-objective and colorless analyses. The Committee of the Associates in Negro Folk Education has no program or thesis of its own and has placed no restrictions upon its authors, opinions and viewpoints through the Bronze Booklet Series, accordingly, the ideas will represent solely those of the respective authors."[62] M. Anthony Fitchue notes:

What gave the conception and publication of the Bronze Booklets an intriguing piquancy was the fact that Locke had tethered together an exciting group of already distinguished African American scholars [Eric Williams, a Trinidadian, was to become the Prime Minster of Trinidad] from the fields of academia, economics, government service, the arts, history, politics, and civil rights, all from ostensibly disconnected universes that in other settings might have immediately collided with some unprecedented force. Scholars with strong opinions such as DuBois only served to strengthen the texture of this bouillabaisso.[63]

There were five Harvard graduates in this group — W.E.B. DuBois, Carter G. Woodson, Ralph Bunche, Sterling Brown, and Alain Locke. The controversy involving DuBois, to be discussed later, raises serious questions about the editorial policy. Unfortunately, the latter aspect of the forementioned editorial policy statement which suggests no particular restraints on authors becomes a central core issue involving DuBois.

A letter from Garnet C. Wilkinson, Treasurer of the Associates in Negro Folk Education to Morse Cartwright, dated 5 March 1935, requested that funds in the amount of $5,250, be transferred to the Associates in Negro Folk Education account.[64] This writer would surmise that this figure was the actual total of grant money received. In a letter to potential authors, dated 1 February 1935, Locke said "the flat honorarium per pamphlet has been fixed at $200, but I shall recommend to the Committee and try to have authorized at least a five or six percent royalty on all sales after the initial printing."[65] In the aforementioned letter, the following instructions are provided to authors:

The booklets are to run in attractive format — size 5 $\frac{1}{2}$ x 8 or 6 x 9 [inches] — from 96 to 112 pages according to the demands of the subject:

that is to say between 27,000 and 34,000 words, including bibliographies and a few pages study outlines with topic references.[66]

The initial cost proposed for the sale of each booklet was $.25. The group of luminaries who were eventually contracted to assume authorship of a booklet was impressive. The authors, titles, and dates of publications are as follows:

Ira Reid, *Adult Education Among Negroes*, 1936
Alain Locke, *Negro and Art: Past and Present*, 1936
Alain Locke, *The Negro and His Music*, 1936
Ralph Bunche, *A World View of Race*, 1936
T. Arnold Hill, *The Negro and Economic Reconstruction*, 1937
Sterling Brown, *The Negro in American Fiction*, 1937
Sterling Brown, *The Negro in Poetry and Drama*, 1937
Eric Williams, *The Negro in the Caribbean*, 1942

The proposed ninth booklet, "Negro History," was never published. The controversy surrounding this omission is discussed later. In addition, it is significant that in his choice of subject areas for the Bronze Booklet Series, Locke did not include religion as a topic; yet in some of his other works, including The Bronze Booklet *The Negro and His Music,* and other writings, he explores the nature and meaning of African American spirituals. Butcher observes the following about Locke's *The Negro and His Music:*

> The spirituals naturally reflect the most serious and intimate aspects of the slave Negro, under the crucible-like pressures of slavery, with semiliterate but deep absorption of the essentials of Christianity; the slave Negro found with remarkable intuition and insight his two main life-sustaining aspirations: the hope of salvation and the hope of freedom. This was creative reaction of the first magnitude; for it did much to save his spirit from breaking. It was also a triumph of folk art. From the episodes and imagery of the Bible, the Negro imaginatively reconstructed his own versions in musical and poetic patterns both highly original and of great emotional vitality. The borrowed materials were transformed to new fervor and a deepened mysticism, stemming very unexpectedly from a naive and literal acceptance of Bible truths and a translation of them into the homeliest, most vividly concrete sort of imagery. Sober evangelical hymns became rhapsodic chants, and the traditional Bible lore came alive again in such new colloquial phrases as "the deep river that chills the body but not my soul."[67]

In each of the published works, Locke provides the reader with biographical information on the author, as well as editorial comments. The following comments taken from Eric Wiliams's work underscore Locke's concern about the role of the United States in achieving global democracy. In the editorial foreword for Williams's work, Locke writes:

> From the racial angle, it is hoped that this study will furnish a closer and sounder bond of understanding between the Negro-American and his brother West-Indian, known all too limitedly merely as a migrant rather than with regard either to his home background or with reference to our common racial history and problems. From the national angle, shared too by the Negro minority, it may also be expected to contribute to a more realistic inter-American understanding and to suggest ways to help — economic, political and cultural collaboration. Both selfishly and altruistically, for national as well as international interest, it behooves the United States to pursue constructive economic and political policies in the Caribbean and without a realistic and objective understanding of the situation and its problems such an enlightened, long-range program is impossible. The issues of this analysis present a challenge to us which, rightly solved, will lead to the constructive enlargement of Western democracy.[68]

In addition to the painstaking editorial forewords, the table of contents presented coherent themes. For instance, in Locke's *Negro and Art: Past and Present,* the sequence of topics is: (1) Negro and Art: Past and Present; (2) The Negro Artist and Negro Art; (3) Early Negro Artists; (4) The Negro Artist Wins His Spurs; (5) Europe Discovers Negro Art; (6) American Art Re-Discovers the Negro; (7) Negro Artists Today; (8) The Negro Through European Eyes; (9) African or Primitive Negro Art; and (10) The Future of Negro Art.[69]

Locke was probably more concerned about articulating the spirituality of African American people and less preoccupied with established religious dogma. African American music, especially spirituals, was his vehicle for exploring the essence of religious underpinnings. In this regard, Leonard Harris's observation is quite apropos:

> Locke was disaffected by the tenets of his family's Episcopalian background and was seeking a spiritual home, one he seemed to have found, at least during the 1920s and 1930s, in the Bahai faith.[70]

Harris also observes that Locke had ultimately been attracted to this faith, which proclaims the spiritual unity of all religions, because he became disillusioned with his family's practice of Episcopalianism.[71] Consequently, Locke's religious experience might be considered atypical in terms of the experiences of African Americans directed at African Americans.

As we witness the growing interest in African and African American art, Locke's booklet, *Negro and Art: Past and Present*, is quite pertinent. African American art, once considered "primitive art" with little aesthetic value, is fast achieving genuine prominence in the larger world. Locke must be given a great amount of credit for launching an aggressive campaign to legitimize African and African American art. He was the first African American major collector of African and African American art, and he encouraged the cultivation of the artistic talents of a number of artists associated with the Harlem Renaissance. Richard Long explains that Locke's interest in African art was "grounded in a profound respect for the African past and for the folk spirit developed in the American South."[72] Therefore, for Locke, "African art presents to the Negro Artist in the New World, a challenge to recapture this heritage of creative originality, and to carry it to distinctive new achievements in a vital, new and racially expressive art."[73]

Why the need for an essay on African American art? Locke passionately felt the need for a response to the European misinterpretation of the works of African and African American artisans. In this Bronze Booklet, he not only extols the mastery of the arts of the feudal empires of Benin, Congo, Senoufo, and other African empires, and explains not only how African art was economically exploited on one level and debased on another, but also chronicles the fecundity of works by African American artists during important historical epochs such as Reconstruction. Locke reveals and exposes how the lack of acceptance of African American artists created a pool of expatriates as well as a group of disillusioned artists, some of whom went to the extreme of taking their lives. Locke believed that those who continued to hone their artistic skills in Europe found greater acceptance of their work upon their return to the United States.

The ultimate stamp of approval by Europeans contributed to the legitimization of black art in this country. Fortunately, the Harlem Renaissance constituted a significant pinnacle in the continuing evolution of African American art. Locke was optimistic about the then new breed of African American artists who evinced a new pride in their heritage. Previously, the African American subject was simply a romanticized figure, at best, or a stereotyped buffoon, at worst; the new artists, however, began to represent a more multifaceted and complex entity in art. Locke's competency to address this subject is supported by Eugene Holmes, a philosopher and former protégé of Locke. He recalls:

> As for himself, he was a true peripatetic, an ambassador, going over much of the western world, telling Europe of Negro art, going to Africa and collecting African art and connecting this with the Negro heritage. He lectured for a year in Latin America and in Haiti. His lecture tours over all America, as guest and visiting professor, also served to make the Locke message about Negro art and the new Negro known to the academic and art world. Being invited to the Harvard Academic Festival in Salzburg in 1950 as a guest professor was a crowning point and culmination in Locke's career.[74]

Richard Long maintains that throughout the 1920s, particularly through the pages of *Opportunity,* published by the National Urban League, "the attention of Alain Locke ranged widely over the areas of Literature, Art, Music, and World Affairs."[75] Locke's essay set the stage for a more comprehensive discourse and pictorial representation of African American art, which is discussed later in this chapter.

The Bronze Booklets, which are still available in print after over fifty years, offer possibilities for continuing discourse about salient and recurring themes on the contemporary landscape. These publications still hold considerable value in the ongoing evolution of Black Studies as a solid, epistemologically-based interdisciplinary field of inquiry.

The premier work in the Bronze Booklet Series was *Adult Education Among Negroes* by Ira Reid, which established a broad context for subsequent booklets. In it, Reid lays out a history of philosophical and historical imperatives for directing specialized efforts toward the facilitation of adult education for African Americans. A professor of sociology at Atlanta University, and former social worker, Reid had a long association with the Urban League, and had participated in studies conducted on African Americans by the W.P.A. Interestingly, Reid shared Locke's vision for adult education — "teaching adults how to live." His essay addresses a number of intrinsic values that should characterize adult education efforts.

As we reflect upon the contemporary implications of Locke's work in 1936, it is indisputable that the art world has come to look more favorably on African and African American art. Even more revealing is the fact that African Americans have become greater consumers of African and African American art, thereby increasing its legitimacy. From a pedagogical and andragogical perspective, African and African American art have emerged as effective and culturally relevant teaching tools for the education not only of African American children and adults, but also of the broader global population.

In *The Negro and His Music*, Locke addresses the contributions of African Americans to contemporary twentieth-century music in the United States. Locke assumed that the African American penchant for music was a result of the need to cultivate or nurture an inherent part of the nature of African Americans. Long asserts that:

> In his essay, "The Negro Spirituals," in the New Negro, Locke gives evidence of his great sensitivity for and knowledge of music. His analytical observations on the spirituals were two generations ahead of any thinking on the subject and are still the most sensitive things said in print that can be understood by the layman.[76]

In *The Negro and His Music*, Locke suggests that the innate rhythm that manifests itself in dance, in turn led to a facility for music. Locke's analysis of the genesis of spirituals and jazz, and the struggle of African Americans to gain acceptance in the more classical/operatic arenas, exposes a recurring and profound theme — race relations. He contends that racism had an adverse effect on the self-actualization of many African American performers. Yet, as Locke suggests, other ethnic groups have reaped the rewards of African American musical prowess. For instance, he cites Jews as being both contributors to and recipients of the heritage of black music, naming Jews such as Eddie Cantor and Al Jolson who had achieved acclaim as minstrels in vaudeville even before the legitimizing advent of jazz. He mentions African Americans such as Ford Dabney, who blazed a trail for Florenz Ziegfield and his famous Ziegfield Follies, creating a revolutionary Negro dance orchestra that was both titillating to watch and sonorous to hear, freely, if not foolishly, relinquished or shared their artistic talents with nonblacks, only to have their seminal contributions ignored.

Ralph Bunche, African American intellectual, statesperson, and the first African American to receive the Nobel Peace Prize, as a special assistant to the United Nations Secretary General's special committee on Palestine in 1947, was subsequently appointed in 1948 to head the United Nation's Palestine Commission. His noteworthy accomplishment was a series of negotiations between Israel and Egypt that led to an Armistice in 1949, for which he was awarded the Nobel Peace Prize. He eventually rose to the position of Undersecretary General of the United Nations in 1955. In *World View of Race*, Bunche addresses and critiques the tenets of anthropology, biology, and the life sciences as they have contributed to what might be viewed as pseudo-scientific bases for the classification of race. In his Bronze Booklet, Bunche posits the idea that race has been used as propagandistic tool for political and economic oppression. The primary thesis advanced by Bunche is expressed in the following excerpt from his booklet:

> It is untrue to say that these hardships were inflicted upon the Negro because of race. More accurately, it should be said that there were certain economic and political forces — the forces of developing industrial capitalism — historically at work in the country which found in the racial characteristics of the Negro a very helpful scapegoat and the persistence of these racial characteristics has meant for the Negro a prolongation and an aggravation of his suffering. . . . Race and race difference alone can never adequately explain the status of the Negro in America.[77]

Bunche continues by challenging the biological basis for race as an argument used by racists to subjugate African Americans. He cautions:

> Racial attitudes are primarily inheritances. In general, they are based on limited and inaccurate knowledge, and are to suit the needs of the dominant. They are certainly not inborn. Small children of different racial stock show no consciousness of race attitudes until they have learned the attitudes of the society in which they live.[78]

We should surmise that Locke shared Bunche's perspectives, for he truly believed in the possibility that attitudes resulting in stereotypes were potential culprits and could only be transformed through education.

The following comments by Jeffrey Stewart raise a specter of inconsistency in Locke's editorial decisions, especially as they relate to the rejection of the DuBois manuscript:

> Although he [Locke] believed Bunche over-stated the case that race was not a factor in modern life, Locke supported Bunche's efforts and published his work. . . . Locke encouraged this new generation [including those politically and ideologically left of center] of historians, economists, and sociologists in his retrospective reviews for *Opportunity* magazine during the 1930s, even though [Locke] cautioned them to appreciate the influence of race and culture if they wished to understand truly the situation of minorities in American colonial world.[79]

T. Arnold Hill maintained a long association with the Urban League, having served as its secretary. In his booklet on *The Negro and Economic Reconstruction,* which incidentally replaced W.E.B. DuBois's manuscript, he emphatically states that irrespective of the early illegality of slavery, the system of indentured servitude became well entrenched in the economic system of the Americas. Hill astutely points out that racism did not predate slavery, but was a product of slavery. Noteworthy in Hill's booklet is an analysis of the promises of Reconstruction and the subsequent role of trade unions in reversing the dismal economic status of African Americans. More importantly, Hill admonished African Americans to acquire self-knowledge and a broader understanding of human relations as an effective antidote for the gnawing sense of inferiority that was one of the deleterious legacies of slavery. Only then would African Americans achieve economic self-sufficiency.

Sterling Brown, a noted professor of English at Howard University and a prolific writer, authored the Bronze Booklets *The Negro in American Fiction* and *The Negro in Poetry and Drama.* Let us first examine his exposition on African American fiction. In this booklet, Brown's critical inquiry is directed at assessing and documenting significant literary works of writers, both black and white, who have written works with black themes within an American setting. He cites writers from the eras of slavery in the United States, Reconstruction, and the early twentieth century. He analyzes enduring themes, such as the plight of the "tragic mulatto" or the "beautiful octoroon lady" with many racial and racist over-tones. More than fifty years later, Toni Morrison, 1994 Nobel Prize in Literature, was to employ similar themes, though from a different perspective. For instance, in her work *Playing in the Dark,* Morrison articulates the following:

The scholarship that looks into the mind, imagination, and behavior of slaves is valuable. But equally is a serious intellectual effort to see what racial ideology does to the mind, imagination and behavior of masters.[80]

In his work *The Negro in Poetry and Drama*, Brown codifies the noteworthy contributions of selected African American poets and dramatists from the period of slavery through the early 1930s. The social and political climates of the times significantly shaped the avenues of expression. Consequently, Brown's primary objectives were to immortalize the then much-ignored contributions of early trailblazing literary artists and to explore the African American themes in poetry and drama. The result is a chronicle of the emergence and evolution of African American artistic expression as revealed in the works of such writers as Phyllis Wheatley and Jupiter Harmon, who had experienced the ravages of enslavement. In addition, Paul Lawrence Dunbar, Countee Cullen, and Langston Hughes, whose works surfaced in a climate of *de facto* segregation and "Jim Crow," are credited with being instrumental in helping to establish a literary tradition in the African American community.

In his discussion of African Americans on stage, Brown exposes the "self-effacing" character of African American minstrel players. More legitimate theater with more meaningful life experience themes did not emerge until the stage production of *Uncle Tom's Cabin* and subsequently, *Porgy and Bess*. Long recounts that Locke had more than a passing interest in drama. He considers the following:

The concern of Locke with the drama was given positive expression in the anthology of plays which he edited with Matthew Gregory. His involvement with the drama was no casual thing. Together with Gregory and Ernest Just, he had been active with the players at Howard University as early as 1912 [over twenty years prior to the publication of the Bronze Booklet Series]. His conception of the role of Drama for the Negro Artist as expressed in the 1927 article, "The Negro and the American Stage," is still unrealized in the consistent practice of any dramatist."[81]

Locke's editorial decision to broaden the scope of the Bronze Booklet Series by extending an invitation to Eric Williams to prepare the manuscript on The Negro in the Caribbean was far-reaching, to say the least. Williams, a political scientist at Howard University at the time and a native of Trinidad, West Indies.

Williams's pamphlet outlines the African's experience in the Caribbean, underscoring the economic exploitation by European nations, including Britain, France, Spain, The Netherlands, and Denmark. It also portrayed the role of the United States in the process of Caribbean colonization. Noteworthy is Williams's analysis of the class/caste system in the Caribbean which characteristically established a legacy of racism in this region.

It is remarkable that following the publication of the first four booklets in 1936, an internal memo of the American Association for Adult Education observed, "prepared by able scholars, these works have a great deal to offer to interested students. One may not agree with the conclusions of the writers, but certainly their treatment of historical material is on a high level. . . ."[82] Morse Cartwright, Executive Director of AAAE, attributed the success of the work of the Associates in Negro Folk Education to the fact that "it has been wholly dominated by competent Negroes."[83] In the same internal memorandum, the following was provided:

> The two pamphlets by Locke deal with Negro art. The author concludes his history of Negro music (booklet no. 2) by pointing to the need of studies of the still untouched sources of folk music (p. 129), and also to the needs of greater cultural opportunities and appreciation of creative musicians. He hopes that the rich art tradition of the Negro which was lost in slavery (booklet no. 3, p. 2) will be revived in the works of younger artists (p. 122). Bunche's work on race is a survey of the scientific knowledge of the subject. His conclusion is that the Negro problem is essentially a class problem; a "solution" will be reached only on strictly economic grounds (pp. 90, 92).[84]

The Bronze Booklets received timely exposure during the 14th Annual Meeting of the American Association for Adult Education held in 1939 in Ontario, Canada, where a special luncheon session was devoted solely to a discussion of the series. At that time, five of the intended eight booklets had been published. The conference theme was "Minorities and Democracy: An Opportunity for Adult Education."[85] This focused session was appropriate and fitting.

The publication of the Bronze Booklets was not without controversy. For example, a conflict arose between Locke and Carter G. Woodson, whose organization, The Association for the Study of Negro Life and History, had objectives similar to those of the Associates in Negro Folk Education. Woodson had been approached by Locke to write the "Negro History" booklet, but Woodson seemed to have refused the invitation because his publishing company, Associated Publishers, would not be the publisher of the booklet. To complicate matters further, Woodson informed Locke of his pending publication, "The Handbook for the Study of the Negro" and invited Locke to "examine" it in his office.[86] The matter was never resolved, despite several exchanges of letters between Locke and Woodson.[87] Finally, Locke approached Schomburg to write the booklet. Sinnette reports, "before the work was completed, Locke and Robert Martin planned to complete the revision of Schomburg's original manuscript. However, the revision was never completed. Thus, eight Bronze Booklets, not nine as originally proposed, were subsequently published."[88]

A second controversy, much more complex, involved W.E.B. DuBois, who had been asked by Locke to write the booklet on what was originally titled "Second Reconstruction." However, according to Russell Linnemann, after accepting the invitation, DuBois requested a change in title to "The Negro and Social Reconstruction."[89] Linnemann has done a creditable job in unearthing the various factions and frictions that surrounded the ultimate rejection of DuBois's completed work. The observations range from discomfort with DuBois's leftist and nationalistic perspectives to his rejection of the New Deal. In addition, I suspect that the Carnegie Foundation had exerted pressure on Locke not to publish the manuscript. However, the central issue which was potentially politically explosive was DuBois's inclusion of what he called the "American Negro Creed," which plotted a course of action for the advancement of African Americans. Eventually, Locke informed DuBois in the following manner:

> It was decided that it would be inadvisable to publish your manuscript "Social Reconstruction and the Negro" largely because of the frequent references to specific situations of public policy.[90]

This apparently contradicts the editorial foreword written for the Bronze Booklets by Locke.

Guy provides an enlightening and candid analysis about what some critics might view as Locke's vacillation on the DuBois manuscript.[91] For instance, he states that Locke argued vociferously on DuBois's behalf, indicating that his primary objection was more one of style than of substance. Yet, in a letter to Lyman Bryson, an influential white member of the advisory team for the Associates for Negro Folk Education, and an influential member of the Executive committee of the American Association for Adult Education, Locke acquiesced in some of Bryson's criticisms of the DuBois manuscript.[92] Those criticisms were clearly based more on substance than style.

Locke advocated for the presentation of different points of view as the editor of the Bronze Booklet Series, yet he shared Bryson's discomfort with "The American Negro Creed" as something of a preamble with nationalistic flavor. The critical question is how far Locke was willing to defend his editorial posture, which would have been ideally strengthened by Bryson with the support of the leadership of the American Association for Adult Education, or the Carnegie Corporation, the funding source.

Talmadge Guy suggests that Lyman Bryson, a professor at Columbia University and a long-time active member and influential leader of the American Association for Adult Education, was likely persuasive in the rejection of the DuBois manuscript. Guy asserts:

> Locke deferred repeatedly to Bryson's judgement on whether certain of the manuscripts, principally those written by Bunche and DuBois, were "pass-

able." Bryson was concerned about the radical perspective — manifest in the case of Bunche and Marxist – Pan-Africanist in the case of DuBois.[93]

In addition, Fitchue suggests that the DuBois manuscript was likely considered propaganda, and thus would not have been timely in light of continuing efforts to seek funds from organizations such as the Carnegie Corporation to support adult education programs."[94] However, I find it rather amazing that Bunche's manuscript was given a "stamp of approval" since Marxism was not embraced by Americans in the 1930s. Was Pan-Africanism considered even more of an internal threat because of its potential to globally galvanize millions of descendents of former enslaved Africans? I would not discount racism; that is, Marxism is more Eurocentrically defined, while Pan-Africanism is, more Afrocentrically grounded. In the case of DuBois, the mingling of Marxism and Pan-Africanism, which had the potential of dismantling barriers to achieving a more integrated and culturally pluralistic global society, made many of his antagonists who were content with maintaining the status quo, quite uncomfortable. Bryson may have been one of those persons.

DuBois was obviously the most controversial among the authors selected by Locke to contribute to the Bronze Booklet Series. For instance, he had been quite vocal in opposing Roosevelt's New Deal. On another level, as a founding member of the N.A.A.C.P., providing stellar leadership, his years of impressive service were nevertheless tumultuous, particularly on issues of ideology and direction. It would be naive to suggest that the latter characterization did not influence the decision not to publish his manuscript. Even some members of the Associates in Negro Folk Education were not comfortable, politically or philosophically, with DuBois. One of DuBois's staunchest critics was E. Franklin Frazier, sociologist, who subsequently published *The Negro in the United States*, which characterized the black family as a "web of pathology," thus preceding Daniel Patrick Moynihan's infamous "benign neglect" attribution.

I encourage the reader to engage in careful reading of the text of "The Basic American Negro Creed," keeping in mind the historical context in which it was written. The following is DuBois's manifesto:

1. We American Negroes are threatened today with lack of opportunity to work according to gifts and training and lack of income sufficient to support healthy families according to standards demanded by modern culture.
2. In industry, we are a labor reservoir, fitfully employed and paid a wage below subsistence; in agriculture, we are largely disfranchised peons; in public education, we tend to be disinherited illiterates; in higher education, we are parasites of reluctant and hesitant philanthropy.
3. In the current reorganization of industry, there is no adequate effort to secure us a place in industry, to open opportunity for Negro ability, or to give us security in age or unemployment.

4. Not by the development of upper classes anxious to exploit the work-
    ers, nor by the escape of individual genius into the white world, can
    we effect the salvation of our group in America. And the salvation of
    this group carries with it the emancipation not only of the darker races
    of men who make the vast majority of mankind, but of all men of all
    races. We therefore, propose this:

BASIC AMERICAN NEGRO CREED

A. As American Negroes, we believe in unity of racial effort, so far as this
    is necessary for self-defense and self-expression, leading ultimately to
    the goal of a united humanity and the abolition of all racial distinctions.
B. We repudiate all artificial and hate engendering deification of race
    separation as such; but just as sternly we repudiate an enervating phi-
    losophy of Negro escape into an artificially privileged white race which
    has long sought to enslave, exploit and tyrannize over all mankind.
C. We believe that the Talented Tenth among American Negroes, fitted
    by education and character to think and do, should find primary em-
    ployment in determining by study and measurement the present field
    and demand for racial action and method by which the masses may
    be guided along this path.
D. We believe that the problems which now call for such racial planning
    are Employment, Education and Health, these three: but the greatest
    of these is employment security in age or unemployment.
E. We believe that the labor force and intelligence of twelve million
    people is more than sufficient to supply their own wants and make
    their advancement secure. Therefore, we believe that, if carefully and
    intelligently planned, a cooperative Negro industrial system in America
    can be established in the midst of and in conjunction with the sur-
    rounding national industrial organization and in intelligent accord with
    that reconstruction of the economic basis of the nation which must
    sooner or later be accomplished.
F. We believe that Negro workers should join the labor movement and
    affiliate with such trade unions as welcome them and treat them fairly.
    We believe that Worker's Councils organized by Negroes for inter-
    racial understanding should strive to fight race prejudice in the work-
    ing class.
G. We believe in the ultimate triumph of some form of Socialism the
    world over, that is, common ownership and control of the means of
    production and equality of income.
H. We do not believe in lynching as a cure for crime nor in war as a neces-
    sary defense of cure; nor in violence as the only path to economic revolu-

tion. Whatever may have been true in other times and places, we believe that today in America, we can abolish poverty by reason and the intelligent use ballot and above all by the dynamic discipline of soul and sacrifice of comfort which, revolution or no revolution, must be the only real path to economic justice and world peace.

I.   We conceive this matter of work and equality of adequate income as not the end of our effort, but the beginning of the rise of the Negro race in the land and the world over, in power, learning and accomplishment.

J.   We believe in the use of our voice for equalizing wealth through taxation, for vesting the ultimate power of the state in hands of the workers, and as an integral part of the working class, we demand proportionate share in administration and public expenditure.

K.   This is and is designed to be a program of racial effort and this narrowed goal is forced upon us today by the unyielding determination of the masses of the white race to enslave, exploit and insult Negroes; but to this vision of work, organization and service, we welcome all men of all colors so long as their subscription to this basic creed is sincere and is proven by their deeds.[95]

I will offer four observations. First, what seems to be a significant contradiction in the creed is DuBois's advocacy of egalitarianism on one hand, and his promotion of an elitist Talented Tenth on the other hand. However, as he suggests in *The Souls of Black Folk*, two "warring" factions inhabit the psyche of the black person. Yet this duality ("Negro" and American) may at times manifest itself as hypocrisy. In actuality, DuBois was sincere in his concern for his people as is evinced by his lifelong record of service and devotion to the cause of African American upliftment.

Second, DuBois's "American Negro Creed" appears to offer some currency to the continuing incendiary social and political conditions in central parts of Africa and the Americas. Most importantly, he points out the necessity for radical social change. Third, these themes echo in contemporary America as they did in the 1930s. Heroes and heroines such as Frederick Douglass and Sojourner Truth, and other African American "troopers" such as Malcolm X and Marcus Garvey, postulated some of the same nationalistic notions as DuBois.

Fourth, Locke, himself, possessed a nationalistic fervor in spite of his seemingly elitist disposition. Many of his writings bear this out. And certainly, his *The New Negro,* which heralded the cultural and aesthetic awakening of the Negro artist and intellectual, has Afrocentric/nationalistic dimensions. For instance, *The New Negro* for Locke represented an unleashing of folk expression and embracing of cultural identity. The result, according to Locke, would be "renewed self-respect and self-dependence."[96] Is that not what DuBois was advocating in the "Negro Creed"? Is that not what Marcus Garvey had earlier envisioned in his "Declaration of Rights of the Negro Peoples of the World," which he had hoped to transform into practice through the work of the Universal Negro Improvement Association?[97] Are those values such as self-respect and self-dependency not some of the same values embraced by more contemporary fringe groups such as the Nation of Islam? Also, Locke suggests that "no one will claim that enhanced group pride and moral self-respect can alone effect a general social transformation, but they are powerful initial factors and must often precede the practical economic and political effort by which group progress is made real and secure."[98] Locke embraced the idea that "cultural activities and their special appeals and incentives enhance the self-respect of the economic group life, urging them toward the transformation of their social and economic conditions to constantly rising levels of security and opportunity."[99] Consequently, it seems incredible that Locke would have difficulty publishing DuBois's "Negro Creed." A possible explanation is that Locke succumbed to the pressure of the existing political climate, including the conservative leadership of the American Association for Adult Education.

Yet, in spite of the potentially volatile situation involving DuBois, the Bronze Booklets, under Locke's editorship, constituted a valuable contribution to the literature of the culture and history of African Americans. Robert Hayden and Eugene DuBois noted that "one of the greatest services which Locke made to the adult education movement was his editorial work on the nine [eight] Bronze Booklets on history, problems and cultural contributions of the Afro-Americans."[100] In fact, the Bronze Booklet Series represented a crowning achievement for Locke and the Associates in Negro Folk Education.

The Bronze Booklets proved to be a rich compendium of historical enlightenment, and they were accessible at an inexpensive cost. They represented a major accomplishment for Locke, who had always insisted that "any emphasis on adult education for Negroes [African Americans], had to be associated with the Negro's past, his culture and his place in America of the post-war period."[101] Thus, these booklets provided rich resources for achieving that imperative, and were an acknowledgment of the value of culture education in bridging the gaps in race relations. Eugene Holmes further observes:

> The success of these Booklets (or reading courses as they were), was enormous. They were on quite a different level from government extension work, the Works Progress Administration projects, the Federal Arts Projects and the Youth Education programs.[102]

Holmes additionally comments:

> These inexpensive booklets sold in the thousands and were in use all over the country, in libraries, high schools, churches, Y.M.C.A.'s and meeting halls.[103]

For Locke, the publication of the Bronze Booklets represented an unabated, continuing effort to provide mass education to the African American community. As a cultural pluralist, Locke likely intended that the booklets reach white audiences whom he would argue needed to be informed about the richness of African American history and culture.

However noble and well-intentioned the mission and purpose of the Associates in Negro Folk Education, they are not above criticism. First, in order to provide intellectual stimulation and ultimately establish the legitimacy of the African American experience in arts and music, Locke carefully selected authors who had achieved noteworthiness in both the African American community and the larger community. This was the *crème de la crème* of African American intellectual and political life. I would also suspect that some, if not all, of the authors viewed the opportunity to be included in the series as a personal achievement that would have broad appeal. Second, during the period when the booklets were published (1936-1941), African American migration continued, bringing with it a host of social, educational, and economic problems for this community. Illiteracy was epidemic, though efforts to address this problem through support of federal/state, private, and community-based organizations were increasing and were showing some flowering. However, an examination of the language of the booklets, raises questions about the intended audience, the masses, who represent endless numbers who could not read. Some scholars point out the success of many enslaved and post-reconstruction free African Americans in mastering the content of the Bible. In spite of the plausibility of that argument, the question remains, were authors guided by their own self-interest and motivation and an opportunity to legitimize their academic and professional expertise in relationship to the larger society, or were they altruistically committed to the struggle of African American empowerment through cultural literacy? Both forces were most likely concurrently operating.

In 1938, two years after the publication of *Negro Art: Past and Present*, one of the booklets in the Bronze Booklet Series, Locke approached the American Association for Adult Education for support of a complementary project, a portfolio of African American art. He envisioned the ideal possibility of including the portfolio in a revised edition of *Negro Art: Past and Present.*

Locke was particularly qualified to engage in this rather unprecedented venture. As Linnemann states, he had become "probably the first American to write perceptively on African Art" and "was among the first major Black American critics and commentators of African and African American Art."[104] Locke's skills in art criticism are evident in the following:

> The best available gauge records not only a new vitality and maturity among American Negro Artists, but a pronounced trend toward racialism in both style and substance: In this down toll of classic models and Caucasian idols, one may see the passing of the childhood period of American

Negro Art, and with the growing maturity of the young Negro artist, the advent of a representatively racial school of expression, and an important new contribution, therefore, to the whole body of American art.[105]

In addition, Locke had encouraged artists associated with the Harlem Renaissance to explore and expand African themes in their work. For example, Sarah Fitzgerald remarks:

His [Jacob Lawrence's] first narrative series, "Toussaint L'Ouverture," received widespread exposure in 1939, when at the urging of Howard University professor Alain Locke, artist Elton Fax, and Harmon Foundation Director Mary Beattie Brady — The Baltimore Museum of Art reserved a separate room for all 41 panels that is a landmark exhibit of African American Art.[106]

In an article by Tribota Benjamin, the artist Lois Mailou Jones notes Locke's influence on her transformation as an artist.[107] Linnemann characterizes Locke as a profound devotee and patron, and a collector who advocated an interdisciplinary study of African art.[108] Unfortunately, the idea of a portfolio on African American art was not initially embraced by Morse Cartwright, Executive Director of the American Association for Adult Education. Cartwright made two glaring observations in correspondence to the Carnegie Corporation, the potential source of funding for the project: (1) "not enough really good pictorial art to make acceptable for publication," was available and (2) "little enduring importance [existed] to glorify in print unworthy art simply because it had originated with Negroes."[109] Cartwright capitulated to the existing sentiments of the day that placed little value on African and African American art.

Locke was determined to challenge the status quo and therefore went directly to the Carnegie Corporation with the blessings of Cartwright, even after the Board of the American Association for Adult Education chose not to take a formal position on the plan. Paradoxically, Executive Director Cartwright had already recommended to Carnegie that the project be declined.

Unbeknownst to Locke, the Carnegie Corporation had sought the expert advice of Alfred Barr of the Museum of Modern Art, who reported his findings of the proposed project:

My conclusion is that a book of carefully chosen works by American Negroes would have some interest and for Negroes especially in schools and in colleges, but the Negro theme in European and American art might well be omitted.[110]

What Barr conveyed was an endorsement of a particular version of African and African American art rather than a universalized perspective. Locke had endorsed the value of both. However, the proposal was initially rejected by Carnegie. Nonetheless, Locke was not to be discouraged in his efforts. Subsequently, in a letter to Carnegie, Locke was forthright and unequivocal. The following excerpt is poignant and profound:

> Oddly enough had the project been framed merely as a record of the work of Negro artists, the major dilemma would have been resolved. But as in the little booklet on "Negro Art," I am committed to the less established position of emphasizing the Negro subject as an art theme rather than the more chauvinistic position of merely playing up the work of Negro the artist. The position that it is wrong to emphasize the color line in art is logically sound and seems to take high moral ground. But it is a pharisee virtue. It denies us as a group, already the victims of an enforced cultural separatism, the positive incentives and residual advantages of a situation which isn't cured by partially ignoring it. The work of the Negro artist needs documentation, and is maturing to a point where it deserves acceptance. Yet, this emphasis in my judgement would be chauvinistic and reactionary if it were not threaded into the broader theme of the development of art of the Negro subject, and in a way to show the collaboration of the white artist in an ever-increasing penetration into the Negro types as subject matter for Native American Art. Social history and tradition have made this paradox: Like Solomon's infant, we have more to lose by being over-logical about it. Better a mis-named baby than a slaughtered innocent.[111]

Locke continues:

> It is strange how hard it is to extend to certain fields precedents already conceded in more traditional areas. Nowhere in art criticism and classification are the denominators logical. Classifications of period, of subject matter, of nationality, of sub-national culture groups are everywhere criss-crossed in critical literature according to shifting interest and emphasis. Christen [Christian] art, Primitive Art, 18th Century Art, Belgian Art, Flemish Art have all become accepted critical categories, though incommensurate with each other. Several of them would seem a paradox if they had not become traditional, but as it is, they are now accepted as critically profitable ways of analyzing art and have become standard in art criticism. This traditional illogic, I contend, is with us on this proposition.[112]

Locke's response to the initial rejection by Carnegie was persuasive since support of the project was eventually facilitated. This was evidently a testament to his resolute spirit. The following excerpt from Locke's introduction to the over-sized volume expresses the timeliness and urgency of this groundbreaking and unprecedented scholarly work:

The Negro's career in the fine arts is little known either to the general or the racial public. There are two reasons for this. One, which this book seeks to help to correct, is the comparative inaccessibility of the materials. The other is a prevalent impression that the fine arts, with their more formalized techniques, are a less characteristic and less congenial mode of expression for the Negro's admitted artistic genius than the more spontaneous arts of music, dance, drama, or poetry.[113]

He continues by providing an historical perspective:

Such views ignore the fact that, although the interactive, emotional arts have been the Negro's special forte in America, his dominant arts in the American homeland were the decorative and craft arts. These — sculpture in wood, bone and ivory, metal-working, weaving, pottery, combined with skillful surface decoration in line and color, involve every category of the European fine arts, even if not in specific terms of the European traditions of easel painting, marble sculpture, engraving and etching. The western world knows today, belatedly, that the Negro was a master artist in the idioms of original culture, and that one characteristic of African virtuosity was in decoration and design. It also admits and admires the vitality and originality of the African art, and judges it almost without peer among the primitive art traditions of the world.[114]

Locke's perspectives are African-centered and respond poignantly to the challenge of correcting myths and distortions about aspects of the African and African American experience. However, Fitchue cautiously notes "that as in fairy tales, Locke's belief that the power of art and literature could overhaul an intractable system of racism was like a belief in ritual magic, leaving any ugly realities to be surmounted, reverses to be endured."[115]

The over one hundred and twenty-five plates contained in the volume present a diversity of mediums (including oil, crayon, tempera, and marble), representing over seventy-five different African American artists. Not surprising is the fact that only nine female artists were cited. Henry Ossawa Tanner, Edmonia Lewis, Hale A. Woodruff, Romare Bearden, Jacob Lawrence, Elizabeth Cartlett, and Charles White were included in the portfolio.

3. National Conferences on Adult Education and the Negro

Locke's ascendancy as a national figure in the adult education movement was squarely catapulted by his leadership in organizing four national conferences on "Adult Education and the Negro," which though held at historically African American colleges, attracted both black and white scholars, professionals, and government workers. These conferences, held at Hampton Institute (later Hampton University), Fisk University, Howard University, and Atlanta University, were jointly sponsored by the American Association for Adult Education, the Associates in Negro Folk Education, and the respective academic institutions. Days observes that though there were eight such conferences, Locke's participation and leadership role in the first three conferences are particularly noteworthy.[116] I have included a fourth conference, since it too was held at an historically "black" college, South Carolina State. Though Locke apparently was not actively engaged in the fourth conference, his sentiments were obviously felt.

The first conference held at Hampton Institute, 20–22 October 1938, had as its theme, "Adult Education and the Negro." It was organized to achieve the following objectives:

1. to portray and evaluate conditions and trends in adult education among Negroes;
2. to discover and make recommendations as to the future development of the work;
3. to consider the place of adult education for the masses in American democracy.[117]

As expected, Locke served as the chairperson of the conference, and William M. Cooper of Hampton Institute served as the director. As Days points out, an impressive list of luminaries included Morse Cartwright, the President of the American Association for Adult Education; Mary McLeod Bethune, then President of Bethune-Cookman College, Ambrose Caliver, Senior Specialist in Education for Blacks, U.S. Office of Education, Lyman Bryson, Columbia University; John W. Studebaker, U.S. Commissioner of Education; and Eugene Kinckle Jones, Executive Secretary, National Urban League.[118]

The two most stirring and profound presentations were apparently those delivered by Cartwright and Locke. In responding to the question, "What Does Adult Education Mean, How Should it be Applied, and Why," Cartwright echoed some of Locke's sentiments:

Without adult education, no true democracy; without democracy, no true adult education. The development of the education and understanding of the individual through free exercise of his will and his intellectual attainment formed the cornerstone upon which democratic government is based.[119]

Locke's topic, "Negro Needs as Adult Education Opportunities," examined the distinct needs of African American adult learners. Though not necessarily advocating radically different types of adult education programs for African Americans, Locke nevertheless posited the following views:

Cultural activities and their special appeals and incentives enhance the self-respect of the people and enable them to assert themselves in healthy fashion in their social and economic group life, urging them on toward the transformation of their social and economic conditions to constantly rising levels of security and opportunity. . . [and education programs for Negroes]. . . to be educationally sound and effective must be kept from the extremes of racial chauvinism. That means that, at the bottom, the racial element must be factually based and soberly balanced instead of childishly emotional or violently partisan. [To achieve effective adult education programs] attention should be devoted to both Black and white at the same time with the same facts and same language. [Moreover,] whites need adult education and in the worst way, as has been aptly put by saying the Black problem is a problem of the white mind.[120]

Locke's appeal for a more global and less racial focus is encapsulated in the following:

We must conclude first that the adult education movement among Negroes cannot maintain itself reasonably or effectively as a separate or special program, even though it is condemned over the large area to separate organization and effort; second, that even with its body in the fetters of a segregated set-up, it must maintain a grasp on universal values and address itself beyond the narrow racial constituency to a general social and cultural service; and, finally, it must align itself with more progressive programs of educational reform and social reconstruction.[121]

A highlight of the conference was a panel discussion on the topic "What Should be the Major Objectives in Adult Education for Negroes?" Vital factors that emerged from this discussion included: (1) "the ability to read and write for oneself is indispensable in American democracy, especially for minority groups like Negroes; and (2) the most pressing problem confronting Negroes is their economic problem but vocational education must be accomplished with political competence." Yet the consensus that emerged from the conference was that "adult education among Negroes should stick close to the fundamental needs of the race, that the test of its worth will be the result obtained in meeting these fundamental needs. This would give culture for culture's sake a secondary place. Vocational and political education should come first."[122]

The conference report delineated six major conclusions and recommendations. They were: (1) adult educators should make every effort to sponsor and encourage the organization of community forums through churches, fraternal organizations, schools, and clubs; (2) attempts should be made to relate the education programs of all agencies to the values that accrue from progressive press information; (3) all colleges, universities, and schools should offer adult education training for all educators; (4) in all fields of adult interest an abundance of simplified materials, comprehensible to adults of third-grade or less reading ability should be made available; (5) the federal and state governments must accept a joint responsibility in making possible needed types of adult education — vocational, academic, and cultural; and (6) the ultimate integration of blacks in all phases of American culture would be the natural outcome of a planned adult education program.[123]

Guy points out that the first conference was characterized by a split among participants on the question, "What should be the foundation and direction of adult education for African Americans?"[124] Locke advocated a culturally-based program, while the majority of conferees advocated a more politically and economically based agenda that would address the practical needs of African Americans. These foci remain critical as we enter the twenty-first century. All seem to be as equally vital now as they were in the late 1930s and early 1940s. Yet the argument about which takes precedence appears less volatile and divisive. Instead, conventional wisdom in the African American community suggests the embracing of a wide range of efforts and directions with the goal of collectively coalescing around broader struggles of liberation and self-sufficiency.

The success of the first conference set the stage for the second national conference that was held at Tuskegee Institute on 22–24 January 1940. The president of the conference was Locke. The conference theme was "The World Crisis and the Negro Masses." The list of notable guests and participants included Morse Cartwright, Executive Director of the American Association for Adult Education; Samuel Madden, Supervisor of WPA Negro Adult Education of Virginia, and F. D. Patterson, President of Tuskegee Institute. Among the topics examined at the conference were "Conditions and Trends in Adult Education Among Negroes," "Problems of Adult Education in the South," "Interracial Emphasis Needed in Adult Education," "Special Training Needed by Adult Education Teachers," and "Extension Work for Adults." In addition, a series of special reports dealt with such issues as "WPA Adult Education Programs for Negroes in Mississippi," "Education Programs in New Jersey," and "Recent Adult Education among Negroes in Texas."[125]

One of the highlights of the conference was Locke's presentation of "Popularized Literature," the theme of which was the infusion of popularized literature in andragogical approaches to teaching the masses.[126] As Days points out, Locke "suggested as one means of popularizing literature among Black learners a 'People's Library,' which would consist of materials that were inexpensive, progressive in points of view, and general in subject matter."[127] Locke's presentation went on to advocate creative use of the radio and phonograph as potentially effective learning/teaching tools. He admonished his audience, "we have had to try to better inform the white constituency with respect to the Negro, but it is certainly just as important and maybe more important to have the Negro constituents well informed about ourselves."[128]

Locke was quite committed to the real or potential role of adult education in influencing the direction of media. The following remarks are poignant:

Do we need to recall the mass irrationalities and excuses of Nazism [and the brutality of the enslavement of African people in the diaspora] to estimate the dangerous potential of social and cultural illiteracy in a modern interconnected world, one, moreover, in which social bigotry and ignorance have access to modern technology for propagating and carrying out their attitudes? As educators, and especially as adult educators, we will do well never to forget this. Control and improvement of the mass mind is now of the utmost importance, particularly if as average reactions show, its current standards are as puerile, irresponsible and reactionary as they seem.[129]

The above observation by Locke is reminiscent of current dangers posed by many right-wing conservative talk show hosts and others in the American media who prey on the racial, ethnic, and gender vulnerabilities of the American public, often perpetuating stereotypes through the use of venomous rhetoric of dissension and divisiveness. However, though the First Amendment to the Constitution provides protection to such individuals, the challenge for those who control the media is to insure that attention is given to portraying individuals and groups with greater accuracy.

Days wrote that one of the major panel discussions at the second annual conference dealt with "Democracy, the world crisis, and the Negro Masses."[130] L. D. Riddick is highly critical of the racist overtones which reverberated throughout this discussion. To make his point, he cites the following divisive comments made by some of the panelists and participants:

"The Negro is a reflection of southern white culture."
"Your suggestion is the best strategy for the Negro: to wait."
"The average Negro perspective is in the south. When he goes north, he wants to come back for burial."
"I don't think there is much hope for them [Negroes] lining up with other minority groups."
"Let's say that from now on, put your case on the white man's conscience and in addition, try ringing the doorbell more persistently."[131]

Yet, the conclusions reached by the panel, were encouraging. They were (1) that blacks would have to see democracy in operation before believing in the ideals of the nation; (2) that the South was one part of the nation where blacks experienced unusual social and economic hardships; (3) that black leadership would have to redefine its tactics and objectives; (4) that legislation on the federal, state, and local levels should be introduced to ensure basic human rights for blacks; and (5) that blacks had developed cultural traditions worth cultivating through adult education programs.[132]

The Third Annual Conference was held at Howard University, 30–31 January and 1 February 1941. This was Locke's turf, for he was Professor and Chair of the Philosophy Department at Howard. Again, Locke had emerged as the president of the conference. The "Foreword" in the conference program noted that the theme of the conference was the "Negro in the National Crisis." In addition to the perennial participants, such as Morse Cartwright and Lyman Bryson, other additional prominent figures were present. They included Robert C. Weaver, Administrative Assistant to the Advisory Commission of the Council on National Defense, who later was to become Secretary of Housing and Urban Development, the first black to hold a Cabinet–level position under the Eisenhower administration, and W. H. Hastie, Civilian Aide to the Secretary of War, who later was to become the first African American judge to serve in the U.S. Virgin Islands. Ralph Bunche also participated in the conference.

In keeping with the general theme of the conference, topics discussed included "Adult Education and Democratic Objectives," "What Adult Education Can Do," "Danger Spots in American Democracy," and "The Negro and National Defense."[133] However, a tremendous amount of conference time was devoted to reports made by an array of representatives from constituency groups such as The National Youth Administration, Negro Workers/Workers Progress Administration, and the Tennessee Valley Authority on Housing Education.

Days selectively highlights some of the outstanding reports.[134] He cites the diligence of the curriculum staff of the Columbia Works Projects Administration in the District of Columbia in preparing a series of readers for teaching adult illiterates. He also notes the work of the Tennessee Valley Authority's Adult Education programs aimed at increasing job efficiency among African American workers.

The "Report of Committee on Findings . . ." concluded the following:

1. That a determined effort should be made to obtain wider representation from agencies now engaged in adult education among Negroes;
2. That a planning committee should be appointed expressly for the purpose of achieving the first recommendation;
3. That fuller participation of the conference membership is greatly desired, especially in view of the fact that excellent reports and addresses have been made by some of the Nation's outstanding thinkers on a variety of subjects of great interest, without adequate provision for discussion of these reports and addresses;
4. That since the conference was so greatly inspired and enlightened by its trip to the Congressional Library to see the special exhibit of Negro Art, the need for more opportunities for seeing adult education in action is recognized, and it is urged, therefore that in the future provision be made for meeting this need.[135]

The findings suggested the need for the expanded inclusion of agencies serving the needs of African American adult learners, for improved levels of participation by conferees in conference deliberations, and for a recognition of the value of observing active program efforts.

A brief word is warranted about a Fourth Annual Conference on Adult Education and the Negro, which was held on the campus of Atlanta University on 5–6 March 1942. The important backdrop is that the United States had entered World War II. Thus, appropriately, the recurrent issue at this conference had to do with the role of the "Negro" in national defense. Readers should bear in mind that we were still dealing with a segregated military.

Consequently, as Neufeldt and McGee point out, one of the significant outcomes that emerged from the conference was "resolved that all discrimination of every type be promptly eradicated from all branches of our armed forces in order that America will be able to say to the world we practice what we preach — we are a democracy in action."[136] Though Locke was conspicuously absent from this conference, the resolution mirrored his constant vigilance in dismantling the vestiges of segregation in this country as a significant dimension of his more global approach to intergroup relations.

Guy's observation is remarkable since it supports the notion that the national conferences confronted critical issues. He offers the following assessment:

> If we take the program of the conferences as a measure, then we can see the concerns of African American adult educators generally. Concerns specific to the African American community were fundamental to all topics during the conferences. However, the aims, goals, types and format of adult education programs discussed tended to be quite diverse.[137]

The above-cited programmatic initiatives, which spanned a period of more than ten years, represent concrete manifestations of Locke's contributions to the adult education movement in this country. Many of the philosophical underpinnings which characterized these programs reflect his philosophical perspectives on values, cultural pluralism, and race relations. Yet, as he engaged in a variety of sponsored adult education related activities, whether as a consultant, speaker, evaluator, author, conference convener, or as a member of special and *ad hoc* committees, one of Locke's recurring themes was the importance of giving of new epistemological meaning to adult education. For instance, he challenged the American Association for Adult Education to examine the scope and meaning of adult education as initially conceived in the 1920s. He keenly, yet satirically, notes:

> Adult Education is the magician's hat of both pedagogy practice and of the educational vocabulary: everything but the appropriate and expected comes out of it; and the more unexpected and inappropriate the developments the more childishly we are. Anything that systematically contacts

adults, almost all varieties of organized propaganda, with the exception of religion and commercial advertising, seem in the judgement of far too many to be entitled to be considered "adult education."[138]

In the following statement, Locke encourages the adoption of meaningful intrinsic objectives:

On this account it is absolutely imperative that before we attempt to consider areas of possible extension and improvement of adult education, we consider very closely the legitimate scope and meaning of adult education itself, without, on the other hand, being unduly doctrinaire. But surely, it should be fairly evident that only the systematic training of adults rather than mere informing, persuading, entertaining or propagandizing of adults is the proper scope of any adult education worthy of the name as serious consideration. It should never be forgotten that "education" is the substantive and thus the substance of the matter, and "adult" merely the adjective reference.[139]

In addition to urging the transformation of the scope and meaning in the provincial areas of adult education, Locke, a cultural pluralist and globalist, insisted that the American Association for Adult Education should extend its horizons beyond narrowly defined missions. He often invoked global perspectives on adult education, underscoring the commonalities among adult learners irrespective of their culture or nationality. The following comments are pertinent:

Our obligation is obvious; our changes of making constructive international contributions challenging. ... The core problem of our field today is ... the development of the most effective techniques of mass education, bold and pioneering experimentation with the new mass media communication to make them serve the social and cultural needs of even larger and larger segments of people ... by radio, motion picture, and visual materials of all sorts, the adult education radius for teaching ... must extend to the new dimensions of an international age. This means more than mere lengthened scope of operations; it means, more critically, the discovery of fresh common denominators of human interests and values, fresh emphasis on the social aspects and implications of knowledge and deeper group attitudes than with mere informational knowledge or individual skills.[140]

The above charge is crucial because it supports the idea that Locke was a visionary. The area of international adult education has become a galvanized effort in bridging the social and economic gaps between developed, developing, and underdeveloped countries in the hemisphere. As a globalist, Locke underscored this theme when he noted that "the adult education radius of teaching must extend to the new dimensions of an international agent."[141] In a more contemporary context, Locke's observation about the critical role of radio and other forms of media is reverberates in the continuing evolution of the Information Superhighway, which holds much promise for mass education. Locke would certainly advocate adult education programs that would insure the inclusion of African Americans in the cybernetic revolution which could potentially and adversely alter the nature of human relations generally, and race relations specifically. Already we have witnessed how this new technology has greatly improved the communications field, yet has also created an opportunity for abuse by unscrupulous consumers who may be prone rather to perpetuate than to resolve racial conflict.

A crowning testament to his charismatic leadership and intellectual acumen was Locke's election as President of the American Association for Adult Education in 1946, at a time when AAAE had achieved a reputation as the flagship adult education organization in the United States. While Locke's election represented a stellar personal accomplishment, also symbolized a growing change in attitude among the membership. To become the first African American to be elected President not only was a singular achievement for Locke, but also represented a political statement for AAAE. Great elation and excitement followed the election. In a letter to Locke, the Executive Director presented the following challenge:

> I want to talk with you at some length about the future of the Association and your relationship to what we plan for next year. We are in the midst of a bull market in adult education and how the American Association can best capitalize upon that presents a problem that is going to demand the best that we can muster in the way of brains.[142]

In the same letter, Cartwright expressed delight at Locke's election. Mary Ely, the Editor of the *Journal of Adult Education* at the time, articulated her unequivocal endorsement of Locke's election in the following manner:

> I am sending warmest congratulations to you as the head of an organization that is united in rejoicing over its new President. I have never seen our members so happy and proud as they were when your election was announced.[143]

A similar letter of congratulations from Frederick Hall, Department of Music, the State Teachers College at Montgomery, Alabama, suggests more than a token gesture on the part of the organization in electing Locke: "Indeed this distinction which you justly earned through your ability and achievement brings honor to our whole race."[144]

At the completion of his year's tenure as President of the American Association for Adult Education, Locke expressed appreciation for having had the opportunity to lead the group, and he commended the membership for its increasing concern about addressing the educational needs of those most in need. He humbly stated:

> Let me hasten to express my deep appreciation and gratitude for the honor which you have bestowed upon me last year in Detroit in electing me your 1946–1947 President. I hardly felt deserving of that honor then and certainly do not now, even after having participated as best I could in the activities of the year. However, I was overjoyed to receive it, and among other things did find some propriety in your symbolic recognition through me of an important objective of adult education — one which I know you will agree with me is basic — namely the necessity of promoting education for the man farthest down.[145]

Though Locke's intellectual interests in adult education were significantly associated with programs sponsored by the American Association for Adult Education, he often assumed a proactive advocacy role in the larger political arena in his efforts to expand cultural education programs in the African American community. A typical example is a correspondence (1935–1936) with the then New York City Mayor, Fiorello LaGuardia.[146] That is, following the completion of a study that explored the needs of the Harlem community, Locke was determined to make a case to the Mayor about the need for improving the quality of life for Harlem residents. In his study, adult education was no less a priority. The initiative is highlighted by the following excerpt:

> A long-range plan of civic improvements in low-cost housing, and slum-clearance, in the further hospital and health clinics facilities, recreation, library and adult education centers, auxiliary school agencies is imperative.[147]

Thus, Locke, who earnestly worked within the system, again demonstrated a penchant for "taking on the system."

Four

THE EDUCATION TRIUMVIRATE:
WASHINGTON, DUBOIS, AND LOCKE

Cultural Democracy is an important and inescapable corollary of political and social democracy, and it involves an open door for the acceptance of minority contributions and for the full recognition of the minority contributions.

Alain Locke[1]

No man who continues to add something to the material, intellectual and moral well being of the place in which he lives is long left without proper reward.

Booker T. Washington[2]

Progress in human affairs is more often a pull than a push, surging forward of the exceptional man, and the lifting of his duller brethren slowly and painfully to his vantage ground.

W.E.B. DuBois[3]

Historically, whenever the topic of the education of African Americans during the post-reconstruction period is broached, invariably the classic Washington/DuBois debate is invoked. As many readers may know, each of these bigger than life figures espoused a contrasting philosophical perspective on the appropriate direction of African American education. Frederick Dunn appropriately characterizes Booker T. Washington and W.E.B. DuBois as embracing an accommodationist or technical skills orientation and radical/integrationist and intellectual orientation, respectively.[4]

Rarely mentioned in the literature is the third, rather inconspicuous member of a seemingly rocky alliance — Alain Leroy Locke. During the zenith of the Washington/DuBois controversy, the primary context for arguments and counter-arguments was Washington's Atlantic Exposition Speech in which he advanced his vocational education program, and DuBois's exposition of the "talented tenth," which he envisioned as a route for achieving political empowerment.[5] Locke, in contrast, advocated a more global and pluralistic approach to education, imbued with a culturally centrist perspective, and has been described as an "arbiter"[6] of the two contrasting philosophies. He saw elements of legitimacy in each of the different perspectives.[6] Locke suggested that it was not a question of either/or, that is, vocational education versus formal academic training for intellectual and political development. For him, each school of thought had its merits as singular approaches.

Locke embraced the Washingtonian philosophy because of Washington's abiding concern about education for the masses, a recurring theme in Locke's formulation of a philosophy of education generally, and adult education, specifically. Though Locke initially endorsed DuBois's concept of the "talented tenth," Johnny Washington postulates that Locke eventually gravitated peripherally to Washington's camp because of the thrust on educating the masses rather than what was perceived as DuBois's apparent focus on educating a "black elite."[7] Locke, like DuBois, argued strongly for the need to educate the best and brightest of the African American community, yet there was another side to Locke's thinking. That is, in the 1930s and 1940s, he turned his attention to the problem of adult mass education. He claimed that in order to improve the conditions of blacks and promote the spread of democracy generally, society had to educate the masses, especially African Americans, who for centuries had been denied adequate education. Eventually, DuBois, as history will reveal, saw the wisdom of this position.

The classical Washington/DuBois debate exposed the haunting question, What should be the proper direction for the education of African Americans? Haywood Burns wisely cautions, "before passing historical judgement, it is well to remember that we are looking at this earlier era through the prism of 1970 [1997]."[8] Prospectively, in the 1990s a renewed interest developed in revisiting the Washington program/agenda for economic development and educational enrichment, as African Americans confronted the continuing crises associated with educational inequities and economic stagnation. Nevertheless, DuBois's program of political empowerment might well be viewed as potentially instructive as the African American community experiences a vacuum in leadership and a widening gap in political enfranchisement.

Though both Washington and DuBois presented sound philosophical justifications for their positions, their practical arguments may have differed. However, they were equally intense and persuasive. Booker T. Washington declared:

> No race that has anything to contribute to the markets of the world is long in any degree ostracized. The opportunity to earn a dollar in a factory just now is worth infinitely more than the opportunity to spend a dollar in an opera house.[9]

On the other hand, DuBois questions the value of conspicuous consumption in the following:

> When turning our eyes from the temporary and contingent in the Negro problem to the broader question of the permanent uplifting and civiliza-

tion of Black men in America, we have a right to inquire, as this enthusiasm for material advancement mounts to its height, if after all the industrial schools is the final and sufficient answer in the training of the Negro
race; to ask gently, but in all sincerity, the ever-recurring query of the
ages, is not life more than meat, and the body more than raiment?[10]

Virginia Denton cites the following pronouncement by DuBois against
Washington's program and Washington's reply:

His [DuBois's] typical complaint was printed in the 12 March 1912 issue
of the Indianapolis *Star:* "We can only come forward through the mind,
not by digging or washing. There is no culture or uplift in washing clothes.
The boys of brain are the wealth of the community." In response to such
public assaults on the Tuskegee programs, Washington replied in custom-
ary fashion, marked "Personal and Confidential," in his papers (vol. II, p.
517). DuBois was "puffed up with insane vanity and jealousy" that deprived him of common sense. "He knows perfectly well I am not seeking
to confine the Negro race to industrial education nor make them hewers of
wood and drawers of water."[11]

According to Denton, the battle lines were drawn. Furthermore, DuBois saw
Washington's educational philosophy as fueled by an apologetic attitude toward white people aimed at maintaining and containing the status quo of segregation. Denton observes:

The Black men of America have a duty to perform a duty stern and deli-
cate — a forward movement to oppose a part of the work of their greatest
leader. So far as Mr. Washington preaches Thrift, Patience, and Industrial
Training for the masses, we must hold up his hands and strive with him,
rejoicing in his honors and glorying in the siren of this Joshua called of
God and of man to lead the headless host. But so far as Mr. Washington
apologizes for injustice, North or South, does not rightly value the privilege and duty of voting, belittles the emasculating effects of caste distinc-
tions, and opposes the higher training and ambition of our brighter minds
— so far as he, the South, or the Nation, does this — we must unceasingly
and firmly oppose them.[12]

However, according to Burns, it was the following disparaging comments
by Washington that propelled DuBois to a level of outrage:

It must not be forgotten that the Tuskegee Machine was not solely the idea
and activity of folk in Tuskegee. It was largely encouraged and given financial aid through certain white groups and individuals in the North.

This northern group had clear objectives, they were capitalists and employers and yet, in most cases sons, relatives, and friends of the abolitionists who had sent teachers into the New South after the war. These younger men believed that the Negro problem could not remain a matter of philanthropy. It must be a matter of business. These Negroes were not encouraged as voters of the new democracy, nor were they to be left at the mercy of the reactionary South. They were good laborers and they might be better. They could become a strong labor force and properly guided they would retain the unbridled demands of white labor, born of the Northern labor unions and now spreading in the South.[13]

Locke attempted to synthesize and integrate the contrasting perspectives of DuBois and Washington:

Education of the mind, heart, and hand, education for social adjustment and practical living, such as the adult education movement envisages, would have become a generally accepted formula for the education of both Black and White and a basis laid down for a truly democratic and democratizing type of education — as indeed it must yet be laid down.[14]

But Johnny Washington appropriately points out:

Thus all three educators — Washington, DuBois and Locke — agreed that education should prepare Black youth [and adults] to assume social leadership in the Black community, but they differed on the means of training. Both Locke and DuBois encouraged Black youth to reject materialistic individualism, an attitude that was so prevalent among Americans and that Washington, some say, encouraged. Washington shared the American economic dream and at the same time encouraged group service. This was one of Washington's paradoxes.[15]

On the other hand, the argument could be advanced that Locke's rejection of materialism was at best lofty, and at worst naive, when considering that the capitalistic grounding of American democracy is embedded in the ideal of "rugged individualism." In terms of the apparent complexity of Washington's position, Burns says:

Washington was not a man without contradictions. While urging his people to concentrate on self-help, and not to be concerned with integration and social equality [the latter of particular concern to Locke and DuBois] he never carried himself as anything less than a full citizen.[16]

Burns extends his characterization of Washington by citing a series of patronage appointments that Washington accepted on various levels of the government. For example, he was the first black assistant Attorney-General of the United States. This observation is rather interesting and somewhat provocative since Washington was consistently opposed to DuBois's call for political agitation around issues of African American political empowerment. Consequently, a legitimate question to be raised is whether Booker T. Washington, chosen as the spokesperson for the African American community, was self-serving.

Marable Manning provides somewhat of an answer to this haunting question when he states:

> The theory of the Talented Tenth was used by DuBois's enemies as proof of his isolation from the masses. In fact, despite Washington's homilies about rural life and the poor, the real elitist was the Tuskegeean. The Tuskegee Machine was comprised of entrepreneurs, editors, small bankers, ministers, and politicians who acted in their material self-interest. Their detente with capitalism hindered the political and economic status of poor Blacks and workers. Frequently they used accommodationist rhetoric simply to win the financial favors of wealthy whites.[17]

Booker T. Washington's position on the direction of African American education is pointedly encapsulated in the following excerpt from his controversial, though, substantive, "Atlanta Exposition" speech:

> Our greatest danger is that in the great leap from slavery to freedom we may overlook the fact that the masses of us are to live by the productions of our hands, and fail to keep in mind that we shall prosper in proportion as we learn to dignify and glorify common labor and put brains and skills into common occupations of life; and shall prosper in proportion as we learn to draw the line between the superficial and the substantial, the ornamental gewgaws of life and the useful. No race can prosper till it learns that there is as much dignity in tilling a field as in writing a poem. It is at the bottom of life we must begin, and not at the top. Nor should we permit our grievances to overshadow our opportunities.[18]

Whether he was conscious of it or not, Washington was indeed embracing an African tradition that can be traced to Songhai, Mali, and Nubia. However, Washington strongly believed that "the agitation of questions of Social equality is extreme folly. . .."[19] Thus, James E. Jackson characterizes Washington as having an accommodationist, capitulationist position, citing Washington's own comments from *Up From Slavery*:[20]

> Let us assure the white folks that their privileges or social equality will not be challenged by us, let them do the voting and have the state governments; let them have the presidencies and chairmanships of all the boards

and institutions. We do not covet the skilled jobs. With such an assurance
the white folk will let us train our hands for the ordinary jobs and we will
survive this age.[21]

Harold Cruse reflects insightfully on the weakness of Washington's economic
plan when he observes:

> Although Washington was understandably echoing the economic free-
> enterprise religion of the twentieth-century American capitalism in black
> terms, it did represent a rather limited panacea for the minority-group
> survival of American blacks. Even a relatively viable black business class
> fostered by Washington's National Negro League would not have gone
> very far alleviating the economic disabilities of the rank and file in the
> industrial, agricultural, and service sectors. This problem exists in the 1980s
> in the efforts of Jessie Jackson's Operation PUSH which is but an updated
> version of Booker T. Washington's Black economic ventures.[22]

Yet, in spite of some stark reservations about Washington's program, Locke
recognized that Washington's idea of vocational education "was original; indeed, in its day it was in advance of American educational reform."[23] Locke
was persuaded that Tuskegee, under Washington's leadership, continued on to
"blaze the trail" of community-wide service projects radiating throughout the
state of Alabama.

Locke both lauded the Washington program and criticized it. The following comments are revealing:

> Booker T. Washington became the symbolic spokesman of Black Recon-
> struction because he advised the Negro to work out his solution in the
> south, and advocated practical, patient self-help pivoted on the gradual
> improvement of the condition of the black masses and the gradual wear-
> ing down of white indifference and prejudice. In its setting — the South
> of Reconstruction — this program was undoubtedly constructive, sound
> and effective. But it did not make concessions with dangerous possibili-
> ties. The Washington program thus became the great divide between the
> conservative and the liberal schools of the race question.[24]

Though Locke respected the thrust of Washington's economic agenda in terms
of black ownership, he abhorred the separatist direction. This is understand-
able, since Locke's philosophy of cultural pluralism idealistically envisioned
an integrated society. Still, Locke had to confront a potential contradiction in
the feasibility and the wisdom of focusing on the teaching of culture subjects to
the majority of African Americans who were confronting the reality of economic deprivation. Johnny Washington offers a thoughtful analysis of this di-

lemma. He says, "to avoid any appearance of his concerns about educating the masses, Locke had to reassess his position on economic issues; which had taken a back-seat to cultural and racial issues."[25] According to Johnny Washington, "the critical dilemma for Locke was, putting it simply, how do you teach cultural subjects, for instance, to groups struggling to survive with menial subsistence. Consequently, Locke's response was to advocate the infusion of cultural subjects in adult education programs that were essentially practical and vocational."[26] Locke fervently believed that such infusion of cultural subjects and materials would "help carry any program to which they are harnessed."[27]

Johnny Washington offers a rather balanced criticism of the classic Washington/DuBois debate, within the context of Lockean axiology, when he posits:

> If Locke's theory is correct, the value orientation of each pulled the Black community into opposite directions. Hence, the conflicts between DuBois and Washington were, by their very nature, irresolvable. At times, both DuBois and Washington acted as though their mandates were issued from God. But in Locke's view, such values are to be understood as being merely preferences and attitudes projected as "absolutes" to which their respective followers expressed loyalty.[28]

I would add that Locke's emphasis on how attitudes are shaped by historical and social contexts helps elucidate the divergent points of view of Washington and DuBois. That is, each provided his own interpretation and analysis within the same historical and social contexts. Yet both were cognizant of a real crisis in American social history. They chose a different path. In more recent times, the Martin Luther King, Jr./Malcolm X strategies for African American empowerment are contemporary echoes of a similar controversy.

DuBois saw the necessity for criticizing Washington but recognized his impact on society. Thus, he declared:

> Today, he [Washington] stands as the one spokesman of his ten million fellows, and one of the most notable figures in the nation of seventy million. One hesitates, therefore, to criticize a life which, beginning with so little has done so much.[29]

Locke obviously saw no contradiction between his support of Washington and his strong identification with DuBois, who initially conceptualized the idea of the Talented Tenth, "whose job it was to inspire and uplift the Black masses."[30] For, as Johnny Washington points out, "they all shared in the American Dream of Progress."[31]

In a speech titled "The Training of Negroes for Social Power," DuBois underscores primary leadership training as a pivotal component of African American education. He comments:

The Negro problem, it has often been said, is largely a problem of ignorance — of the world and its ways, of the thought and experience of men
[and women]; and ignorance of self and the possibilities of the human
souls. This can be gotten rid of only by training; and primarily such training must take the form of that sort of social leadership which we call
education. To apply such leadership to themselves, and to profit by it,
means that Negroes would have among themselves men [and women] of
careful training and broad culture, as teachers and teachers of teachers.[32]

A direct linkage appears between DuBois's comments and the following
observation by Locke regarding the critical role of service and leadership in the
African American community:

If there is anything specifically traditional and particularly needed in
Negro education it is the motive and ideal of group service. And though
the loss of it in the more capably trained Negro of the present generation
is partly due to the prevalent materialistic individualism of middle class
American life, a still larger loss is due to an inevitable and protective
reaction against the present atmosphere of education.[33]

DuBois's eventual reconstruction of the Talented Tenth concept, originally considered elitist, is outlined in the following:

My Talented Tenth must be more than talented, and work not simply as
individuals. Its passport to leadership was not alone learning, but expert
knowledge of modern economics as it affected American Negroes; and in
addition to this and fundamental would be its willingness to sacrifice and
plan for such economic revolution in industry and just distribution of
wealth, as would make the rise of our group possible.[34]

The above utterances by DuBois are significant for these reasons. First, they
signal somewhat an infusion of Washington's thrust on economics. Second,
DuBois's statement represents a broader socialistic perspective on the crises
and challenges faced by the African American community. Third, and equally
significant is the observation that DuBois eventually shifted the responsibility
of leadership from a Talented Tenth to a broader representation of the masses,
including fraternal and service organizations. Stewart further explains:

DuBois's modification of his conception of the Talented Tenth grew out
of his growing realization that transformation of the economic system
deactivated many of the sources of social unit among Blacks which he
had assumed earlier to be inviolable. DuBois had originally seen the emergence of the Negro group leader which, in the aggregate comprises his

"Talented Tenth" as a potential substitute for the submerged African heritage of Blacks thrust into the American capitalist environment.[35]

Though Locke seemed to endorse the original basic tenets of the Talented Tenth, his perspectives were more global and inclusive than those of DuBois. Johnny Washington suggests that Locke's recruitment of the Talented Tenth was inclusive because "it is consistent with his support of contacts and social reciprocity among leaders of all ethnic groups in order for democracy to work in America."[36] DuBois is quite clear about the racial background of his Talented Tenth, when expounding the following:

> The Negro race, like all races, is going to be saved by its exceptional men. The problem of education, then, among Negroes must first of all deal with the Talented Tenth; it is the problem of developing the Best of this race that they may guide the masses away from the contamination and death of the Worst, in their own and other races.[37]

Rather than from a racially defined elite group, as in the case of DuBois, Locke spoke from a broader human resources perspective when he referred to an "aristocracy of talent," which he envisioned as a beacon of hope for the preservation and realization of democratic values.[38]

Days notes that in his article on the Talented Tenth, Locke was not advocating an elitist concept of education as an end in itself, but as a means of providing needed leadership in working toward improving the educational status of the black masses.[39] He was convinced that a cadre of trained educators was needed to plan and implement adult education programs that would address the issues of black illiteracy, despair, unemployment, and the health problems which were rampant in the black community.

The key role of economics in the scheme of things was recognized early by Booker T. Washington, and subsequently by Locke, who believed that if economic disparities had been revolved "an educational reconstruction had as yet to be accomplished would have been successfully inaugurated."[40] Thus, Johnny Washington concludes that "by calling attention to economics, Locke seemed to share Booker T. Washington's concerns."[41]

Quite remarkable was DuBois's eventual position that the economic and self-help thrust of Washington's philosophy had real merit. Burns observes that even six or seven years after Washington's Atlanta Speech, DuBois said, "the day the Negro race courts and marries the savings bank will be the day of its salvation."[42] Cruse emphasizes that "without ever admitting that Booker T. Washington had indeed been closer to the truth in 1900, DuBois switched his attention to the problem of economic self-sufficiency."[43] The reader should bear in mind that DuBois had initially raised the following issue in objecting to Washington's philosophy:

Is it possible that nine millions of men can make effective progress in economic lines if, they are deprived of political rights, made a servile caste, and allowed only the most meager change for developing their exceptional men? If history and reason give any distinct answer to these questions, it is an emphatic no.[44]

Locke's embracing and ultimate synthesis of both schools of thought are consistent with his philosophical objection to absolutes. In his "Values and Imperatives," Locke states, "our varied absolutes are revealed as largely the rationalization of our preferred values and imperatives."[45] He further observes that "their taproot, it seems, stems more from the will to power than from the will to know. Little can be done, it would appear, either toward their explanations or their reconciliation on the rational plane." Also, his middle-of-the-road position served as a buffer between the contrasting perspectives held by DuBois and Washington. Locke seems to have mastered the art of conflict resolution as far as Washington and DuBois were concerned. On that point, Johnny Washington observes that Locke "represented the effort to synthesize the opposing ideas of Washington and DuBois."[46] Thus, Locke's inclination to arbitrate without compromising the essence of their principle tenets and to mediate and synthesize points of view are consistent with his axiology that value conflicts by their very nature are irrevocable. The challenge according to Locke is to find ways to control such value conflicts "by understanding how and why, to find principles of control from mechanisms of valuations themselves."[47]

During the post-reconstruction period in this country, defining and plotting the education terrain for both African American youth and adults were of paramount concern for most African Americans and some whites. In an atmosphere of continued prejudice and discrimination, high illiteracy rates, and a plethora of economic and political imperatives, the stage was set. Consequently, many African American voices emerged, including those of Frederick Douglass and Carter G. Woodson. However, the most historically enduring discourse on the issue of African American education involved the classic debate between Booker T. Washington and W.E.B. DuBois. The intercession of Locke as an arbiter and synthesizer of the contrasting schools of thought greatly influenced by Locke's philosophical thrust on more global, intrinsic values, suggested that a key goal of education should be a tolerance for differences in a culturally pluralistic society. For Locke, room existed for both the vocational/technical orientation of Washington and the more academic and intellectual orientation of DuBois.

Adult education for Locke seemed a natural and appropriate avenue for addressing the needs of those who had been liberated physically from enslavement and had endured the oppression of "Jim Crow," finding themselves ill-equipped socially, psychologically, economically, and educationally to live in a society plagued with inequality, injustice, and racism. Surely, scholars and others will continue to examine and critique the salient philosophical and pragmatic ideals of Washington and DuBois. I would suggest that the contributions of Locke should add another critical dimension to this historical drama.

Irrespective of some stark differences and some commonalities among the triumvirate, some lessons are to be learned as we confront contemporary issues about the general state of education in the United States, and more specific discourses about multi-cultural and multi-ethnic education and Eurocentric/Africentric epistemologies. Washington, for instance, advocated the acquisition of vocational skills as critical to the realization of self-sufficiency, a cry echoed by Malcolm X and other proponents of economic development of the African American community. Yet Malcolm X recognized the nature of political empowerment espoused by DuBois as is evident in "The Ballot or the Bullet," one of Malcolm X's powerful speeches.

Though he initially advocated for the creation of an elitist leadership class who would educate the masses in the ways of political empowerment, DuBois eventually acknowledged that leadership would have to evolve from the masses. This position echoed the position of Marcus Garvey at that time, and later the position of Malcolm X. Prior to his deportation in 1928, Garvey was scheduled to visit Washington in Tuskegee. He had embraced Washington's economic empowerment programs. Johnny Washington observes that Garvey "encouraged them [African Americans] to build their own economic, political and cultural institutions and to do so independently of the white society, whose values, practices, and institutions he considered corrupt."[48] Through his organization, the Universal Negro Improvement Association, Garvey focused on the cultivation of African American leadership from the bottom-up.

The Washington/DuBois debate has received the attention of a broad range of intellectuals and political activists, and over the years, scholars have intermittently revisited this controversy in an effort to generate, for example, alternative contexts for analysis in an effort to evolve new insights. However, the following observation by Burns is quite instructive:

> If historical judgements are to be passed, they should be placed in the context of the times. Booker T. Washington, for all his ability and behind the scenes maneuvering, misjudged his times. He was never able to understand the effect of change from an individualized, agrarian economy to a mass industrial economy. His training program depended upon individual skill and craftsmanship already quite out of step with the contemporary American economy. At the same time, he placed too much faith in the white South's willingness to encourage and support black progress. DuBois, in contrast, was something of a prophet. He understood his times and the need to protest. More than this, his analysis remains valid today. Through his key role in challenging Washington and in organizing the Niagra Movement and the N.A.A.C.P., DuBois may properly be seen as the Father of the modern protest movement. Although Washington died in 1915 and the Armenia Conference the following year, resulted in a truce

in the great debate, DuBois continued until his death in 1963 to raise his voice of protest in opposition to those who would counsel accommodation. Indeed, in Black leadership circles, in one form or another, the Washington/DuBois debate continues today.[49]

Burn's observation is biased in the direction of vilifying Washington and glorifying DuBois.

Notwithstanding, two events shed light on the leadership issue. First, the Armenia Conference, held in Armenia, New York in 1916 and sponsored by the N.A.A.C.P., was an effort to address some serious leadership problems in the organization, which had been greatly influenced by a solid cadre of white leadership. It brought together a highly diverse group. The center of controversy was DuBois and his possible elevation to the position of executive secretary, thus insuring a stronghold on the editorship of the *Crisis*, the official organ of the N.A.A.C.P. Second, David Levering Lewis observes that Booker T. Washington had died the week before the conference, thus, leaving some to believe that the DuBois/Washington controversy was put to rest. Yet, Lewis, quite insightfully places the controversy in a reasonable perspective by explicating that:

> The controversy was really not about DuBois and Washington in an ultimate sense, and would have emerged inevitably in one form or another. Essentially, the Talented Tenth and the Tuskegee Machine were responses by two African American leadership groups to white supremacy as it existed in two regions of the United States. In that sense, Washington's impoverished, agrarian South, with its monocrop economy and biracial demographics, was no fit arena for the high-minded cultural and exigent civil agenda of the people for whom DuBois spoke. Conversely, the lowest- common-denominator realities and patient abnegation embraced by Washington was no program for racial advancement in the urban, industrial multiethnic North. DuBois and Washington, in speaking for two dissimilar socioeconomic orders, were really speaking past each other rather than to the same set of racial problems and solutions; but DuBois, for all his Victorian sensibilities and elitism, had the advantage of speaking to the future, while Washington, business-oriented and folksy, spoke, nevertheless, for the early industrial past.[50]

In contrast, Denton aptly places Washington's philosophy in historical context:

> Washington's era of leadership occurred from 1866 to 1920, the greatest period of democratization and maturation of the United States and of the country's adult education movement. As the nation's attention turned more to common people and practical education in agriculture, worker's educa-

tion, and industrial education, schools, colleges, libraries, and museums also proliferated. Washington's quest for the acculturation of former slaves through education reflected the national tenor evidenced in other signifi-cant crossroads of history, such as the Americanization of immigrants at the turn of the century.[51]

It is absolutely correct to state that the debate goes on. However, as we continue to examine and redefine the appropriate direction of African American edu-cation in a contemporary atmosphere that focuses on cultural diversity and multi-cultural paradigms, the Lockean culture factor might again serve to broaden the scope of the debate.

All of these bigger than life figures were gadflies in their own right. Booker T. Washington was aggressive in formulating a strategy and agenda for the up-lifting of the African American community in an atmosphere of extreme racial intolerance following reconstruction. His self-help economic plan has contem-porary import as many global communitees in the African diaspora continue to confront the vestiges of colonialism, racism, and economic disparity. DuBois was imbued with a profound desire to "shake-up" the political system by em-powering African Americans with, for instance, the effective use of the vote. Is this not a continuing challenge in the African American community, in spite of gains in the numbers of African American elected officials? Those meager gains have not significantly revolutionized the educational, criminal justice, and other economic and political systems that continue to inflict various forms of geno-cide on the African American community.

Locke's emphasis on culture and cultural reliance has borne fruit. African Americans have become more African-centered in both their attitudes and be-haviors, embracing rather than rejecting their African heritage. Yet Locke's notion of tolerance, which according to Johnny Washington might be perceived as "live and let live,"[52] resulting in a de-emphasis of the need for social change. Instead, many who have embraced the image of the "New Negro," an African-centered persona, have been vilified on some levels.

Thus, all three educators — Washington, DuBois, and Locke — agreed that education should prepare black youth to become adults who would assume social leadership of the black community, but they differed on the means of training. Both Locke and DuBois encouraged black youth to reject materialistic individualism, an attitude that was so prevalent among Americans and that Wash-ington, some say, encouraged. Washington shared the American economic dream and at the same time encouraged group service. This was one of Washington's paradoxes.

The historiography of the classical Washington/DuBois debate paints a canvas of two powerful and influential African American leaders who were almost completely at odds with each other. Yet, as Burns observes, "contrary to the solution put forward, the two men were not always diametrically opposed

philosophically."[53] Remarkably, six or seven years after Washington's Atlanta
Speech, evidence exists their of evolving mutual respect. Burns highlights
Washington's favorable reply to DuBois's request to teach at Tuskegee, in spite
of the fact that DuBois had accepted another position by the time he received
Washington's reply.[54] Indeed, a subsequent offer was made to DuBois, though
he declined. Another observation made by Lewis is worth considering.[55] He
explains that in several instances Washington supported DuBois in his futile
efforts to obtain employment. A case in point is DuBois's attempt to become
the Assistant Superintendent of the District of Columbia Public School system
in 1900. That is, the Assistant Superintendent slot reserved for "colored"; a
comparable slot was reserved for "whites." The titular head or superintendent,
who was white, had persuaded DuBois to apply.

While Washington may have wavered at some point in his support, he at
least gave the outward appearance of being supportive of DuBois. DuBois was
not successful in his bid to secure the position. I suspect that Washington's
initial support was diluted by the likely influence of DuBois's opponents.

DuBois did not always passionately denounce Washington and his pro-
grams. Occasionally, he displayed expressions of admiration and respect for
Washington, which may be perceived as giving some degree of credibility to
Washington's agenda for achieving economic self-sufficiency in the African
American community. Denton maintains that Washington's fight against segre-
gation on the railroads was supported by DuBois.[56]

The explosive political issue on which Washington and DuBois were
firmly in agreement is identified by Burns.[57] For instance, he observes that as
late as 1899 neither Washington nor DuBois subscribed to the ideal of universal
suffrage, practically insisting that some form of qualification be applied. Since
in many parts of the country, particularly the South, qualifications to vote included the passing of a literacy test, the need for adult education, whatever its
form or fashion, was tied inextricably to suffrage.

Locke's mediating role in the Washington/DuBois debate was to be
demonstrated even in what has been described as his magnum opus, *The Negro
in American Culture*, which was published posthumously. The following excerpt encapsulates a fundamental pragmatic difference in perspective between
Washington and DuBois that surely impacted on the shaping of their educational philosophies:

> Too often, the American mind, lacking knowledge of these facts (e.g.,
> slavery constituting a mockery of democracy), and so without proper his-
> torical perspective on American slavery, follows the great cover-up tradi-
> tion that makes the Negro bear the blame as well as the brunt of the situa-
> tion; often it is assumed that his very presence in the body politic has

constituted the peace problem. Booker T. Washington's shrewd pleasantry that Negroes were the only element of the American population which came by special invitation, passage paid, has scarcely sufficed to drive home the sober realization that the Negro was desperately needed and humbly but importantly effective in the settlement of the New World. His warrant for being here is beyond question, doubly so because his mass service of basic labor in the wide zone of the slave system was unrewarded for seven or eight generations. In his *Gift of Black Folk,* W.E.B. DuBois rightly rates the Negro's labor as his first substantial contribution. No matter how the benefits be reckoned, it remains a fact that the Negro's begrudged share in American civilization was dearly bought and paid for in advance of delivery.[58]

For Locke, educating for cultural literacy would constitute a driving force in eliminating this disparity.

Five

LOCKE'S CONTEMPORARY IMPORTANCE AND UNIVERSAL APPLICATIONS OF LOCKEAN PHILOSOPHY OF ADULT EDUCATION

A race of people is like an individual man; until it rises on its own talent, takes pride in its own history, expresses its own culture; affirms its own self-hood, it can never fulfill itself.

Malcolm X[1]

Alain Leroy Locke has been referred to as a "Drum Major," a "Cultural and Social Mentor," and a "Renaissance Man." Beyond these characterizations, Locke was not just a "man for all seasons," assuming concurrent roles as a teacher/philosopher/mentor, race relations expert, Afrocentrist, aficionado of African art, and adult educator; but his fecundity in all of these areas of interest was realized with equal vigor.

Throughout his illustrious career, Locke was affiliated with a host of organizations that were either committed to educational change and reform or to confronting the complex issue of race relations in this country. The list is endless. The following are important: American Negro Academy, American Society for Race Tolerance, American Council on African Education, American Council on Education/Committees on International Education and Cultural Relations, Committee for African Students in North America, Council on African Affairs, Bureau for Intercultural Education, Negro Society for Historical Research, and African Union Society of Oxford. These organizational citations in no way encompass the numerous *ad hoc* committee memberships and consultative roles that Locke engaged in until his untimely death.

The strong degree of integration and coherency among all of Locke's intellectual and professional pursuits reflects a profoundly humanistic perspective. His conception of the "New Negro" which laid the foundation for the formulation of the essence of African American aesthetics, was reflected in his agenda for educating African American adults, a program that emphasized the infusion of history and cultural subjects. On another, more abstract level, his philosophical ideas about values imperatives constituted a fundamental element in his philosophical posture about intrinsic values in adult education.

Just as in the case of the celebrated Washington/DuBois debate, I would argue that any criticism of Locke's agenda for the education of African American adults must be grounded in an appropriate historical context. That is, Locke's involvement in the adult education movement occurred from the mid-1920s through the late 1940s, a time in which we witnessed the emergence of a black middle class, and the evolution of a culture of poverty among the masses of African Americans who were confronted with the ravages of Jim Crow, segregation, and other forms of dehumanization that made a mockery of democracy. As separate and distinct strategies, the DuBois and Washington plans for African American "upliftment" did not constitute a panacea for the mass education of the African American community. This is not to suggest that there were not some positive and effective dimensions of their agendas. For instance, Black entrepreneurship appeared and a growing sense of heightened political consciousness was spurred by such organizations as the N.A.A.C.P. under the leadership of DuBois.

Locke provided an alternative paradigm — culture-based education, which requires some degree of scrutinization as well. First, the teaching of cultural-based subjects may threaten to divert attention from the social realities that relate to economic and political survival. Yet, if integrated into technical/vocational programs, as Locke argued, it would have its greatest impact. How this integration might occur is not clearly articulated by Locke. Second, it is dangerous to de-emphasize the practical value of mastering basic reading and writing skills in a communication-driven society in which communication skills become the measuring rod for both economic and political opportunity and equality. A case in point is the continuing plight of hopeful job seekers who cannot successfully complete an employment application. Achieving political parity requires an ability to comprehend the language of politics. Third, Locke invokes the idea of mass education, indicating a gravitation away from his shared sentiment with DuBois in focusing on the so-called Talented Tenth.

It is not clearly established who benefitted from the adult education programs for which Locke provided impetus and direction. Was it truly the masses of African American proletarians, or the middle class, who had already achieved some semblance of comfort economically and politically. On this point, we might question the intended audience for the Bronze Booklets, written by African American intellectuals, each conveying his own professional style and language, which might have exceeded the comprehension level of many African Americans at that time. Yet, the booklets were probably culturally validating and self-affirming for others. Not to be disregarded is the recurring issue of "Black English" or Ebonics which surfaces on the education landscape every ten years or so. The issue of Ebonics presents an interesting irony; that is, in retrospect, the language we call "Black English" or Ebonics characterized much of the poetic and literary works of the Harlem Renaissance, of which Locke was a leader. The literary works that emerged from the Harlem Renaissance were hailed as exemplary, and certain of these works are now considered valuable contributions to the literary canon in this country. In Lockean terms, they were culture-based and validated the essence of African American history and culture in this country. Consequently, I would surmise that if alive today, Locke would endorse the idea of Ebonics as a positive incentive for greater acceptance and mastery of so-called standards.

In spite of real or perceived flaws in Locke's perspectives on the education of African American adults, he consistently challenged educators to address the problem of race relations. For example, he argued:

> The paramount need in these days of increased racial tension and of augmented interracial and international concern over the issues of race is to comprehend the major and important trends of thought and action involved. As an intellectual problem the primary demand is for clarification; and this indeed, is probably the role of education in the situation and the main constructive contribution the educator can make to the total situation. There is as much need for the right perspective on these basic matters of human group relations as for the right information or even the right moral principles and convictions.[2]

The importance of intrinsic values in the African American community is fully addressed by Locke in the following:

> There is little need for giving any statistics about how many Negroes there are in the United States and about what their problems are, their hopes, and their aspirations. Really we already know the Negro's basic desire is to be able to live freely anywhere that he chooses and to have the same opportunity for developing culturally and physically and economically as is permitted any other citizen. Therefore, instead of considering these statistical aspects, let us look at the problem of living that the Negro faces. First of all, more so than any other racial minority, the Negro must look two ways in attempting to live what has been called in religious education the full life. He must be objective in that he must see the same goals that other Americans see. He must strive for them; he must use the same tools and devices for realizing these goals. He must also be subjective, in that he cannot reach the goal that he desires so long as he sees his racial brethren forced to submit to the lower planes of living patterned for Negroes in the United States. On the one hand he must be a free individual, revering all the ideals of the nationality group, and on the other hand he must be a tolerant and a servile individual who knows his place.[3]

In terms of the focus of this book, Locke's contributions to the education of African American adults might cast him as a maverick, or even in some respects, a social agitator. First, though he was generally acquiescent to the broad agenda of the adult education movement, he was diligent and unwavering as he sought to augment and adapt those broad agenda items to the needs of African American adults. Second, whether consciously or unconsciously assuming the role of provocateur in a white hierarchical leadership inner circle, Locke's mere presence might in some respects epitomize the conscience of African Americans, long denied opportunities to, in Locke's words, "learn how to live." Needless to say, for an African American intellectual during the 1920s and 1930s, gaining acceptance was often accompanied by manifestations of tokenism. In retrospect, we might be inclined to label Locke as a "token" in unchartered waters; yet, rather than acquiescing to any such moral indignation, Locke used his academic training and highly respected credentials as weapons for change.

Both philosophical and practical themes repeat in Locke's writings and speeches, whether they focus on adult education or more formal, traditional education (that is, specifically higher education). These themes include: (1) the need for parity in education; (2) the value of teaching culture-based subjects; and (3) more globally speaking, engendering tolerance and respect for differences and underscoring the imperative of values in achieving a culturally puralistic society. First, Locke's position on parity is well articulated in his essay "Negro Education Bids for Par." In it, he advocates a compensatory approach to education for African Americans, who were long excluded from quality educational opportunities. Johnny Washington recalls:

> Throughout most of his writings, Locke claimed that education at all levels — elementary, secondary, college and adult — should be organized on the principle of cultural and ethnic reciprocity in order to further understanding among the world's diverse groups.[4]

Also, Locke placed some accountability on black colleges in regard to assuming responsibility for narrowing the gap, by providing social leadership in the African American community. For instance, in a commencement address at Fisk University, he exhorted the graduating class to:

> Abandon or seriously revise your notion of success and turn it from the materialistic and personalized values of rugged individualism into the socialized and more humane values of contributing to the common welfare.[5]

This mandate truly reflected certain aspects of Locke's axiology in calling for a transformation of attitudes.

Second, Locke was unbending in insisting on the value of teaching cultural subjects across the education spectrum. For within the context of his views on cultural pluralism, this was especially critical for African Americans, but equally important for white students whose images of African Americans have often been tainted by stereotypes such as "coon," "stepin-fetchit," and "Amos and Andy."

Third, inherent in Locke's axiology is the need for greater tolerance and mutual respect for differences, with the goal toward a democratic society which truly unites many as one. Since elementary and secondary schools had failed to achieve this end, Locke envisioned adult education as a channel for the ultimate realization of this goal.

The African American–centered philosophical underpinnings of Locke's agenda for African American adult education is well captured in the following:

> Let us, then, take the Negro case merely as a special instance of a general problem requiring special attention and effort, perhaps, because of its acute degree but in its significance and bearing upon educational problems and methods considered diagnostic and universally applicable. The condition of the Negro and its educational implication will fit and parallel any similarly circumstanced group and, in addition, like many other acute situations, will point the lesson of new and generally applicable techniques.[6]

Guided by his philosophical perspectives on the importance of values and values imperatives, as well as cultural pluralism, Locke envisioned adult education not merely as a conduit addressing the rampant problem of illiteracy among African Americans, particularly during the great southern exodus to the northern urban hamlets from 1915 through the 1930's, but also as a platform for transforming global attitudes that grew out of stereotyping and xenophobic machinations. Douglass Stratford offers the following clarification:

> But Alain Locke was not a Negro addressing himself exclusively to a Negro audience. To read his dissertation, *The Problem of Classification in a Theory of Value* . . . is, I think to see that he might well have said the same kind of thing to any people.[7]

Yet Charlotte Morgan underscores Locke's unquestionable influence in creating a greater sense of race pride in the African American community. She explains:

> Alain L. Locke, philosophy professor at Howard University, played a pivotal role in developing a rationale for race consciousness which was acceptable to most Black educators. While a Rhodes Scholar, he formulated a program to develop a Black self-respect and pride through reconstructing African tradition. His objectives, elaborated on in 1925 were, first, the attainment of American ideals and institutions, and second, the correction of the damaged group "psychology" and reshaping of a warped social perspective. Once created, this new group psychology would lead to more positive self-respect, self-reliance, self-direction. Subsequently, the system of tutelage and social dependency which shackles Blacks would be

thrown off. Locke's race consciousness was not anti-American. It was, rather, a way to make known all attributes of American culture so that they could be more fully shared. Consequently, racial assertiveness was a focus of many adult education programs.[8]

For Locke, cultural literacy was no less important than learning basic reading and writing skills. He believed that in order for African Americans to survive and prosper in a pluralistic society, they had to first know their history and culture. If African Americans were to attain the "full life" in terms of opportunity and freedom, Locke insisted that they "must be objective in that he [they] must see the same goals that other Americans see; and subjective, in that he [they] cannot reach the goals he [they] desires so long as he [they] sees his [their] racial brethren forced to submit to the lower places of living patterned for Negroes in the United States."[9] This admonition parallels many of the Kwanzaan principles which have become manifest in the African American community as guiding principles for social, political, and economic survival.

In many respects, the Kwanzaan principles are reminiscent of the philosophical underpinnings of the social, political, economic, and educational tenets espoused by Booker T. Washington, W.E.B. DuBois, and Alain Leroy Locke.[10] The principles of Ujima (Collective Work and Responsibility), Ujamma (Cooperative Economics), and Kujichagulia (Self-determination) echo many elements of Washington's philosophy of African American economic survival. DuBois would have been quite comfortable with the principles Umoja (Unity), Kujichagulia (Self-determination), Kuumba (Creativity), and Nia (Purpose). His "American Negro Creed" reflects many dimensions of those principles.

Locke's work was often imbued with symbolic as well as practical manifestations of such principles as Kuumba (Creativity), Imani (Faith), and Kujichagulia (Self-determination). Kuumba resonates throughout Locke's ground-breaking work, *The New Negro,* which makes a persuasive case for the necessity for African Americans to embrace their own folk culture as a prerequisite for creative self-expression. The Harlem Renaissance became a conduit for the programmatic implementation of these principles, to the timeless credit of Locke, one of the principal movers and shakers of that artistic movement. However, in spite of his insistence on collective efforts among African Americans, Locke's speeches and writings frequently reveal themes that underscore the responsibility of democracy to dismantle the shackles of injustice and inequality. For Locke, African Americans had paid their dues both by presevering in the monumental struggle for freedom and by participating honorably in the futherance of American democracy.[11]

Locke was very much a political activist and advocate, often finding himself engaged in the political arena. On a national level, he supported the New Deal, to the dismay and chagrin of DuBois who saw the New Deal as counterproductive to African American economic and political self-sufficiency. On a more local level, a specific example is his involvement in the politics of New York City following the infamous Harlem riots in the 1930s. Locke exchanged correspondence with Mayor Fiorello LaGuardia in which he advocated a comprehensive cultural arts center in Harlem as one means of addressing declining conditions and services in the Harlem community. LaGuardia had some familiarity with Locke as a result of Locke's publication "Harlem: Dark Weathervane," which interested LaGuardia because of its criticism of the city's indifference to the Harlem community.

In a confidential report to the Mayor, Locke emphasized the recurring theme of the importance of culture in the upliftment of African Americans. He wrote:

> Harlem needs a boost to its morale and will rise to a dramatic overture from City Hall that will go beyond the Harlem Report. In this situation I can think of nothing more constructive . . . than the immediate sponsoring of a plan for a civic art and recreation center for Harlem. [Harlem needs] a community center. It should consist of at least an entire city block and include a public auditorium for concerts, theatricals, etc.; rooms for exhibits of arts and crafts, etc., classrooms and workrooms for child and adult education.[12]

Locke saw the teaching of democratic values to be central to the role of adult education for African Americans. Andragogy would be a tool for empowerment. Concurrently, Locke felt that a meaningful andragogical agenda would be infused with the teaching of cultural subjects. He felt that African Americans could not effectively and meaningfully participate in the democratic process if they were not grounded in a knowledge of their history and culture, which historically was denied them. Consequently, cultural literacy had to precede economic and political self-sufficiency. Thus, Locke's preoccupation with intrinsic values in adult education evidently is a consistent theme.

Though Locke's visibility and connection to the Harlem Renaissance and his ultimate conceptualization of "The New Negro" has received more attention in the literature than his involvement in adult education, there is clearly some consistency and continuity between his philosophy and leadership in both movements. In both instances, Locke was driven by the need to transform the image and status of African Americans.

Locke discusses in the following appraisal the need for creating a pedagogy (andragogy) that would address the social chaos in the African American community:

> As a group we have had relatively more leisure than either native American peoples but have utilized it along personal rather than social lines. Today, at the time when leisure is tending to become more democratic and at the same time more social, we are finding it necessary to equip ourselves for a new way of living. At one time it was a matter of jobs being taken away.

At another, the question of relief. At another, taking care of transient workers. Because approximately one-half of our population shifted its place of
residence from rural to urban centers during the last twenty-years, it has
become necessary to readjust our social institutions. The church no longer
fulfills the full social needs of the group. The missionary society is no longer
adequate enough to care for the relief population. Our moral code no longer
places an important ban upon dancing or card playing, and they have in
many instances become accepted forms of diversion. But in education we
are following the same old rut. As individuals we are expanding rapidly but
our organizations and institutions failed to keep pace. It is out of this chaos
that the ideas for an adult education program among Negroes evolved.[13]

Locke's philosophical bent toward racial and ethnic group tolerance was well
entrenched, at least, idealistically, in his hopes and aspirations for a meaningful
content for adult education in the lives of people. He makes the following points:

But we are wisely coming more and more to regard the responsibility for
the proper conditioning of individual and group opinion with regard to
social attitudes and behavior as a problem of an educational character,
even though it forces us to realize how much more important the informal
and adult stages of our educational effort necessarily become in this instance as even against the strictly formal and preparatory stages of our
education. It is not too utopian, however, to assume that as we correct the
deficiencies of the social education aspects of formal education there will
remain much less to be done [and undone] by informal adult education
efforts. In this we confront perhaps the greatest aspect of the racial situation: the emergency character of the present-day situation with its crucial
and critical urgencies.[14]

The teaching of tolerance for differences was of paramount concern to
Locke. He envisioned one of the missions of adult education to be that of teaching respect for individual and group differences. He observed:

We have not progressed very far toward better social integration, or saner
social understanding, or more healthy social participation through our objective study of history and sociology and abstract political science. Nor
have we promoted unity or tolerance by our educational policy of ignor-
ing differences and stressing uniformity. Indifference has been the usual
result of this procedure.[15]

The current educational debates raging on the landscapes of the educational turf across this country under the banner of diversity, multi-culturalism,

and Afrocentric versus Eurocentric philosophical underpinnings, echoes and reverberates many of the philosophical and pragmatic issues previously confronted and explored by Locke. This suggests that possibly our refusal, resistance, or inability to tackle serious educational problems during the early part of this century have reappeared as demanding challenges for educational reform in the 1990s and well into the twenty-first century.

The legacy of Locke may well provide insight into relevant ideas about how we might attempt at another point to address complex educational issues. More specifically, as we search for more viable epistemological alternatives to interpreting the African American experience, I would advise contemporary pundits of "Black Studies" or African American–centered education to engage in a serious analysis of Locke's scholarship, which embodies Afrocentric themes and perspectives. Linnemann quite appropriately remarked:

> Certainly the explosion of interest in Black studies in this country over the last twenty-five years accounts in good measure for the interest in Locke's observations about these topics.[16]

Laypeople and scholars alike have been deeply concerned with the search for a black identity, the formulation of a black aesthetic, and an elaboration of the black cultural experience. Locke was an early pioneer and pivotal shaker not only in focusing attention on these issues and concerns, but in creating an intellectual context for an African worldview. Though sometimes perceived as an elitist, Locke was committed to the idea of an African-centered education. The publication of the Bronze Booklets is a case in point.

Was Locke the premiere Afrocentric adult educator of the twentieth century? If we consider Asante's definition, one might venture to respond affirmatively. That is, Molefi Asante posits the idea that the context for viewing phenomena is grounded in the experiences of the African person, as opposed to phenomena being viewed from the perspective of the experiences of Europeans.[17] Furthermore, Asante's paradigm places the students as the subjects rather than the objects of education, which is comparable to Greg Thomas's observation that black people of African descent become the narrators, not the narrated.[18] Given this framework, Locke's profound immersion in cultural pluralism which provides a philosophical anchor for the contemporary multi-cultural movement, places him in a dubious position since the notion of Afrocentrism may be viewed as antithetical to the idea of multiculturalism. Yet Greg Thomas suggests that the concepts are "complementary and not antagonistic."[19]

The Afrocentric nature of Locke's philosophy is comparable to that of some contemporary African American scholars. For instance, William Cross, Jr., who has written extensively on "regressive theory" (the process of internalizing one's Africanness), establishes an identification with Locke as he quotes the following from *The New Negro*.

In the last decade something beyond the guard of statistics has happened in the life of the American Negro and the three norns who have traditionally presided over the Negro problem have a challenge in their laps. The Sociologist, the Philanthropist, the Race-leader are not unaware of the new Negro but they are at a loss to account for him. He simply cannot be swathed in their formulae. For the younger generation is vibrant with a new psychology; the new spirit is awake in the masses, and under the very eyes of the professional observers is transforming what has been a perennial problem into the progressive phases of contemporary Negro Life (Locke, 1925).[20]

The archives containing Locke's work in the field of adult education generally, and African American adult education specifically, have barely been scratched. They await the intellectually curious and those educators and teachers who manifest a real concern about exploring possible solutions to the growing illiteracy rate among African Americans, the high school drop-out rate, escalating unemployment and underemployment, and the unpredictable impact of welfare reform. As we struggle to advance beyond the rhetoric of multicultural education to the theory-building and practice that embody culture-centeredness, we need to revisit Locke, in terms of his legacy as it impacts on the contemporary American landscape and the heightened importance that many African Americans are giving to cultural and historical literacy. This distinguished though incomplete list includes Leonard Jeffries, Yosef ben-Jochannan, John Henrik Clarke, Molefi Asante, Frances Cress Welsing, John Hope Franklin, Malauna Karenga and Cornel West.

In the African American communities across the country, study groups, lecture series, and the like, have sprouted up in our churches, community centers, art galleries, and museums. They suggest that we have come full circle, since these activities were critical dimensions of the Harlem (especially) and Atlanta Experiments in Negro Adult Education which heralded the richness of the African history and tradition. The availability of books, pamphlets, and the proliferation of other forms of media productions directed at the African American community were of utmost importance to Locke. He saw these channels as critical to the spread of mass education generally and pivotal in imparting cultural education, specifically. The latter part of the twentieth century has witnessed a growing urgency in the African American community to know and to document its culture and history. African American scholars and others are influencing the publishing empire, and African and African American art continue to gain greater acceptance, respectability and poignancy, thereby, transforming the culture and politics of the art world and generating an expanded pool of enlightened African American consumers of African American art and artifacts. A hunger for self-affirmation is clear. African Americans are expanding their worldview through travel, for instance, to the "mother-land," often returning with a broader view of their place in the world. Is it possible that African American adults have begun to respond to Locke's appeal? Regardless, the challenge remains of educating African American youth to learn, to know, and to embrace their culture and history as necessary armor for their economic and political survival as adults.

Linnemann described Locke as a "renaissance man."[21] Washington reminds us of Locke's view of himself as a "philosophic midwife."[22] More importantly, Locke believed that philosophers have a responsibility to deal with the problems that history produces, thus, underscoring his commitment to the practice of philosophy. This observation somewhat parallels West's observation that "an academic usually engages in rather narrow scholarly work, whereas, an intellectual is engaged in the public issues that affect large numbers of people in a critical manner."[23] By this definition, Locke was an erudite, intellectual visionary, who not only dreamed of the possibilities for improving the human condition, but actively and vigilantly sought to alter the state of race relations in this country. For Locke, adult education was a major channel for achieving those ends. What was to be Locke's magnum opus, *The Negro in American Culture,* was completed after his death by Margaret Just Butcher, daughter of Ernest Just, one of Locke's closest friends and colleagues. In the introduction to the text, Butcher captures the purpose of the book:

> . . . to trace in historical sequence but topical fashion — both the folk and the formal contributions of the American Negro to American culture. It aims further, to trace and interpret the considerable influence of the Negro on American culture at large. Its main thesis is that by setting up an inveterate tradition of racial differences in the absence of any fixed or basic differences of culture and tradition on the Negro's part, American slavery introduced into the very heart of American society a crucial dilemma whose resultant problems, with their progressive resolution, account for many fateful events in American history and for some of the most characteristic qualities of American culture. On all levels, political, social, and cultural, this dilemma has become the focal point, descriptive as well as constructive of major issues in American history.[24]

Thus, Locke's interpretation of American social history generally, and yet specifically underscoring the significant role of African American history and culture, provides a kaleidoscopic overview of the education of African American adults.

A final observation is appropriate and timely. What we know about Alain Leroy Locke as a person is superficial, and therefore provides limited insight. No definitive biography has been written. Though a renewed interest in Locke as a philosopher is evinced, for instance, by the formation of an Alain Locke Philosophical Society under the auspices of the American Philosophical Society, a more in-depth exploration of his persona might result in a profound analysis of how his personal attributes affected his work in plotting the direction of African American adult education far into the future.

NOTES

Guest Foreword

1. Alain Locke, "Negro Needs Adult Education," in *The Philosophy of Alain Locke: Harlem Renaissance and Beyond,* ed. Leonard Harris (Philadelphia: Temple University Press, 1984), p. 56.

2. Alain Locke, " Frontiers of Culture," *The Crescent: Official Organ of the Phi Beta Sigma Fraternity,* 33: 1 (1950), p. 37.

Chapter One

1. David Levering Lewis, *When Harlem Was in Vogue* (New York: Oxford University Press, 1981), p. 149.

2. Douglass K. Stafford, "Alain Locke: The Child, the Man, and the People," *Journal of Negro Education*, 30 (1961), p. 25.

3. Rayford W. Logan and Michael R. Winston (eds.), *The Dictionary of American Negro Biography* (New York: Norton, 1983), p. 398.

4. Leonard Harris (ed.), *The Philosophy of Alain Locke: Harlem Renaissance and Beyond* (Philadelphia: Temple University Press, 1989).

5. *Ibid.,* p. 145.

6. Horace Kallen, "Locke and Cultural Pluralism," *The Journal of Philosophy,* (28 February 1957), p. 123.

7. Harris, *The Philosophy of Alain Locke*, p. 6.

8. *Ibid.,* p. 5.

9. Johnny Washington, *Alain Locke and Philosophy: A Quest for Cultural Pluralism* (New York: Greenwood Press, 1976), p. 23.

10. Harris, *The Philosophy of Alain Locke,* p. 7.

11. Cornell West and bell hooks, *Breaking Bread* (Boston: South End Press, 1991), p. 29.

12. Alain Locke, "Enter the New Negro," *Survey Graphic*, 53 (1925), pp. 633–634.

13. Richard Long, "Alain Locke: Cultural and Social Mentor," *Black World* (November 1970), p. 90.

14. Elinor Des Verney Sinnette, *Arthur Alfonso Schomburg: Black Bibliophile & Collection* (New York: New York Public Library & Detroit: Wayne State University, 1989), p. 45.

15. Malcolm Knowles, *A History of Adult Education in the United States* (Malibar, Fla.: Robert E. Kreiger Publishing Company, 1977, revised).

16. Harvey G. Neufeldt and Leo McGee (eds.), *Education of the African American Adult* (N.Y.: Greenwood Press, 1990).

17. Harold Stubblefield, *Towards a History of Adult Education in America: The Search for a Unifying Principle* (London: Croom Helm, 1988).

18. Robert Hayden and Eugene DuBois, "A Drum Major for Black Adult Education: Alain Locke," *The Western Journal of Black Studies*, 1 (December 1977), pp. 293–296.

19. Everett Alston Days, "Alain Leroy Locke (1886-1954): Pioneer in Adult Education and a Catalyst in the Adult Education Movement for Black Americans" (Ed.D. dissertation, North Carolina State University at Raleigh, 1978).

20. Talmadge C. Guy, "Prophesy from the Periphery: Alain Locke's Philosophy of Cultural Pluralism and Adult Education" (Ed.D. dissertation, DeKalb: Northern Illinois University, 1993).

21. Russell J. Linnemann (ed.), *Alain Locke: Reflections on a Modern Renaissance Man* (Baton Rouge, La. : Louisiana State University, 1992), p. 14.

22. Washington, *Alain Locke and Philosophy,* p. 23.

23. Elizabeth A. Peterson (ed.), *Freedom Road: Adult Education of African Americans* (Malabar, Fla.: Kreiger Publishing Company, 1996). The two noted essays are: La Verne Gyant, "Alain Leroy Locke: More than an Adult Educator," and Talmadge Guy, "The American Association of Adult Education and the Experiments on African American Adult Education."

24. Alain Locke, "Areas of Extension and Improvement of Adult Education," *Journal of Negro Education*, 14 (1945), p. 453.

25. Alain Locke, The Need for a New Organon in Education, Proceedings of the *Ninth Symposium Conference on Science, Philosophy, and Religion* (New York: Harper and Brother, 1950), pp. 201–221. Also, see Leonard Harris, ed., *The Philosophy of Alain Locke: Harlem Renaissance and Beyond* (Philadelphia: Temple University, 1989), pp. 263–278.

26. Logan and Winston, *Dictionary of American Negro Biography,* p. 401.

27. Guy, "Prophesy from the Periphery: Alain Locke's Philosophy of Cultural Pluralism and Adult Education," p. 89.

28. See any issue of *Journal of Adult Education.*

29. Linnemann, *Alain Locke: Reflections on a Modern Renaissance Man*, p. 2.

30. Mark Helbling, "Alain Locke: Ambivalence and Hope," *Phylon,* 40 (1979), p. 294.

31. Harris, *The Philosophy of Alain Locke*, p. 22.

32. Long, "Alain Locke: Cultural and social Critic," p. 89

33. Washington, *Alain Locke and Philosophy*, pp. 3–4.

34. Eugene Holmes, "Alain Locke: Philosopher, Critic, and Spokesman," *The Journal of Philosophy*, 54:5 (28 February 1957).

35. A. Gilbert Belle, "The Politics of Alain Locke," *Alain Locke: Reflections on a Modern Renaissance Man,* p. 53.

36. Logan and Winston, *Dictionary of American Negro Biography,* p. 401.

37. Linnemann, *Alain Locke: Reflections on a Modern Renaissance Man*, p. 4.

38. Eugene C. Holmes, " Alain Locke and the Adult Education Movement," *Journal of Negro Education*, 34 (Winter, 1965), p. 7.

39. Hayden and DuBois, "A Drum Major for Black Adult Education: Alain Locke," p. 45.

40. Washington, *Alain Locke and Philosophy*, p. 146.

41. *Ibid.*, p. 23

42. Leonard Harris, "Identity: Alain Locke's Atavism," *Transaction of the Charles S. Peirce Society* (1968), p. 68.

43. *Ibid.,* p. 69.

44. Alain Locke, "Cultural Relativism and Ideological Power," *The Philosophy of Alain Locke: Harlem Renaissance and Beyond*, ed. Harris, p. 73.

45. Alain Locke, "Values that Matter," *Key Reporter,* 19 (May 1954), p. 54.

46. Alain Locke, "Negro Needs As Adult Education Opportunity," *The Philosophy of Alain Locke*, pp. 257–258.

47. *Ibid.*

48. Stubblefield, *Towards a History of Adult Education in America, Introduction.*

49. Knowles, *A History of Adult Education in the United States,* p. 36.

50. Neufeldt and McGee, *Education of the African American Adult*, p. 26

51. Knowles, *A History of Adult Education in the United States.* Preface.

52. Stubblefield, *Towards a History of Adult Education in America, Introduction.*

53. *Ibid.*

54. *Ibid.*

55. See Lyman Bryson, *Adult Education* (New York: America Book Co., 1936).

56. See Huey Long, *New Perspectives on the Education of Adults in the United States* (London: Croom Helm, 1987).

57. See Eduard C. Lindeman, *The Meaning of Adult Education* (Montreal: Harvest House, 1961, original publication 1926).

58. Alain Locke, "Areas of Extension and Improvement of Adult Education," *Journal of Negro Education*, No. 14 (1945), p. 453.

59. *Ibid.*

60. Linnemann (ed.), *Alain Locke,* p. 11.

61. Holmes, "Alain Locke: Philosopher, Critic, and Spokesman," p. 7.

62. Alain Locke, "Coming of Age," *Adult Education Journal* (January 1947), p. 3.

63. Alain Locke, "Pluralism and Ideological Peace," *Freedom and Experience,* ed. Milton Konvitz and Sidney Hook. (Baltimore: Cooper Square, 1975, reproduction of original 1947 publication). Also, see Leonard Harris, ed., *The Philosophy of Alain Locke.*

64. Guy, "Prophesy from the Periphery," p. 182.

65. *Ibid.*

66. Alain Locke, "Negro Needs as Adult Education Opportunities," *The Philosophy of Alain Locke,* ed., Leonard Harris, p. 256. Also, see Locke Papers, Moorland-Spingarn Research Center, Washington, D.C. and *Findings of the First Annual Conference on Adult Education and The Negro* (Hampton, Va.: Hampton University Press, 1938).

67. Alain Locke, "Minorities and the Social Mind," *Progressive Education*, 12 (March 1935), p. 143.

68. Alain Locke, "Education for Adulthood," *Adult Education Journal*, 16 (July 1947). Quoted from William Townsend, "Toward Full Equality," *Adult Education Journal*, 5 (October 1946), pp. 105–106.

69. Washington, *Alain Locke and Philosophy*, p. 143.

70. Locke, *Enter the New Negro*, p. 633.

71. Alain Locke, "Areas of Extension and Improvement of Adult Education," *Journal of Negro Education*, 14 (1945), p. 453.

72. *Ibid.*, p. 455.

73. Sinnette, *Arthur Schomberg: Black Bibliophile and Collector*, p. 170.

74. Alain Locke (ed.), *The New Negro: An Interpretation* (New York: Albert and Charles Boni, 1925).

75. Lewis, *When Harlem Was in Vogue*, p. 149.

76. Steven Watson, *The Harlem Renaissance* (New York: Pantheon Books, 1995), p. 25.

77. Molefi Asante, *Kemet, Afrocentricity, and Knowledge* (Trenton, N.J.: African World Press, 1990), p. 95.

78. Alain Locke, "Intellectual Interests of Negroes," *Journal of Adult Education*, 8 (June 1936), p. 352.

79. *New York Times (*10 June 1954), p. 31.

80. "The Passing of Alain Locke," *Phylon,* 15 (1954), pp. 243–252.

81. *Ibid.*

82. *Ibid.*

83. *Ibid.*

84. Eugene Holmes, "The Legacy of Alain Locke," *Freedomways*, 3:3 (1963), p. 306.

Chapter Two

1. Alain Locke, "Negro Needs as Adult Education Opportunities." from a speech delivered at the *Findings of the First Annual Conference on Adult Education and the Negro*, (Hampton, Va., 20-22 October 1938).

2. Alain Locke, "The Coming of Age," *Journal of Adult Education*, 6 (1947) p. 3.

3. Alain Locke, "Trends in Adult Education for Negroes," (speech delivered at the annual meeting of The American Association for Adult Education) Locke Papers, Moorland-Spingarn Research Center, (Washington, D.C., 22 May 1940).

4. Malcolm Knowles, *Applying Modern Principles of Adult Learning* (San Francisco: Malcolm S. Knowles Associates, 1984), p. 6.

5. Malcolm Knowles, *The Modern Practice of Adult Education: From Pedagogy to Andragogy* (rev. ed.) (Chicago: Association Press, 1980).

6. Daniel D. Pratt, "Andragogy as a Relational Construct," *Adult Education Quarterly*, 39:3 (1988), p. 160.

7. Locke Papers, Moorland-Spingarn Research Center, Washington, D.C.

8. John Hope and Mae Hawes, "Need for Adult Education," *Fundamentals in the Education of Negroes,* ed. Ambrose Caliver, (Washington, D.C.: U.S. Department of Interior, Office of Education, 1935), p. 67.

9. Alain Locke, Untitled Speech, 25th Anniversary of AAAE, Locke Papers, Moorland-Spingarn Research Center, Washington, D.C.

10. *Ibid.*

11. *Ibid.*, pp. 2–3.

12. *Ibid.*

13. Ira Reid, "The Development of Adult Education for Negroes in the United States," *Journal of Adult Education*, 14 (Summer 1945), p. 304.

14. Locke, "Negro Needs as Adult Education Opportunities," *The First Annual Conference in Adult Education and the Negro* (Hampton, Va.: Hampton Institute Press, 1938), p. 7.

15. Locke Papers, Moorland-Spingarn Research Center, Washington, D.C., p. 2.

16. See Paulo Freire, *Pedagogy of the Oppressed* (New York: Continuum Press, 1970); and Paulo Freire, *Educating for Critical Consciousness* (New York: Continuum Press, 1973).

17. Alain Locke, "Trends in Adult Education for Negroes," Locke Papers, Moorland-Spingarn Research Center, Washington, D.C., pp. 6–7.

18. *Ibid.*

19. Alain Locke, "The Role of the Talented Tenth," *Howard University Record,* 12 (1948), p. 14.

20. Alain Locke, "Negro Needs as Adult Education Opportunities," Locke Papers, Moorland-Spingarn Research Center, Howard University, Washington, D.C., p. 7. Also, see Leonard Harris, ed., *The Philosophy of Alain Locke,* pp. 253–262.

21. *Ibid.*

22. Locke Papers, Moorland-Spingarn Research Center, Washington, D.C. Also see *Survey Graphic* (January 1947), pp. 87–89.

23. Locke, "Trends," p. 5.

24. Locke, "Negro Needs," p. 8.

25. J.A. Atkins, "Special Training Needed by Adult Education and the Negro," (Tuskegee, Ala.: Tuskegee Institute, 1940), pp. 29–36.

26. Alain Locke, "Popularized Literature," *Findings of the Second Annual Conference on Adult Education and the Negro*, pp. 48–50.

27. Locke Papers, Moorland-Spingarn Research Center, Washington, D.C.

28. David Joseph Burgett, "Vindication as a Thematic Principle in Alain Locke's Writings on the Music of African Americans," *The Harlem Renaissance: Revaluation* (New York: Garland Publishing Inc., 1989), pp. 140–141.

29. Alain Locke, "Areas of Extension and Improvement of Adult Education Among Negroes," *Journal of Negro Education*, 25 (Summer 1945) p. 455.

30. Alain Locke, "Education for Adulthood," *Adult Education Journal*, 6 (July 1947) p. 104.

31. Alain Locke, "Negro Needs as Adult Education Opportunities," in Harris, *The Philosophy of Alain Locke,* p. 255.

32. Alain Locke, "Trends," pp. 2–3.

33. See Howard Gardner, *Multiple Intelligences* (New York: Basic Books, 1993).

34. Johnny Washington, *A Journey Into The Philosophy of Alain Locke* (Westport, Ct.: Greenwood Press, 1994).

Chapter Three

1. La Verne Gyant, "Contributions to Adult Education: Booker T. Washington, George Washington Carver, Alain Locke, and Ambrose Caliver," *Journal of Black Studies*, 19:1 (September 1988), p. 103.

2. Eugene C. Holmes, "Alain L. Locke and the Adult Education Movement," *The Journal of Negro Education*, 34 (Winter 1965), p. 6.

3. Alain Locke, "Adult Education: Safeguard and Democracy," speech delivered at the Southeastern Regional Conference of the American Association for Adult Education (Locke Papers, Moorland-Spingarn Research Center, Washington, D.C., undated).

4. *Ibid.*

5. Everette Alston Days, "Alain Leroy Locke (1886-1954): Pioneer in Adult Education and Catalyst in the Adult Education Movement for Black Americans," *Dissertation Abstracts International,* No. 79-055-02.

6. Ira Reid, *Adult Education Among Negroes* (Washington, D.C.: Associates in Negro Folk Education, 1936), p. 21.

7. Elinor Des Verney Sinnette, *Arthur Alfonso Schomburg: Black Bibliophile & Collection* (New York: The New York Public Library & Detroit: Wayne State University Press, 1989) p. 171.

8. Ira Reid, *Adult Education Among Negroes*, p. 21.

9. *Ibid.*

10. Harvey G. Neufeldt and Leo McGee (eds.), *Education of the African American Adult* (New York: Greenwood Press, 1990), p. 121.

11. Ernestine Rose, "Report of Harlem Adult Education Experiment to Mr. Cartwright for the Year 1932," Schomburg Center for Research in Black Culture, Countee Cullen Library Collection, Box 2, New York.

12. Sinnette and Hopper to Anderson, 15 July 1932, Report on NYPL grant X733 11 November 1931, Carnegie Corporation Grant Files, Columbia University Library, New York.

13. Sara E. Reid, *Harlem Adult Education*, National Conference on Fundamental Problems in Education of Negroes, Washington, D.C., 9-12 May 1934.

14. Ira Reid, *Harlem Adult Education*, p. 33.

15. Charlotte Morgan, "More than the Three R's: The Development of Black Adult Education in Manhattan," *Adult Education in a Multi-Cultural Society*, ed. Beverly Cassaria (New York: Routledge, 1990), p. 68.

16. Rose, *Report of Harlem,* p. 15.

17. Days, *Alain Leroy Locke,* p. 96.

18. *Ibid.*, p. 97.

19. See "Snapshots of the Atlanta Experiment in Adult Education Among Negroes," Auburn Avenue Research Library on African American History and Culture, Atlanta, October 1931-August, 1932, p. 4.

20. Days, *Alain Leroy Locke*, p. 99.

21. Eliza Gleason, *The Southern Negro and the Library* (Chicago: University of Chicago Press, 1941), p. 45.

22. Ira Reid, *Adult Education Among Negroes,* p. 28.

23. Gleason, *The Southern Negro*, p. 46.

24. Sara E. Reid, *Harlem Adult Education*, p. 29.

25. *Ibid.*

26. Letter from William Hale, Jr. to Mae Hawes dated 15 September 1934, Auburn Avenue Research Library on African American History and Culture, Atlanta.

27. Letter from B.E. Anderson to Mae Hawes, dated 17 November 1934, Auburn Avenue Research Library on African American History and Culture, Atlanta.

28. See "Snapshots of the Atlanta Experiment in Adult Education for Negroes."

29. Letter from Dorothy Jones, Secretary to Mae Hawes, dated 4 January 1934. Auburn Avenue Research Library on African American History and Culture, Atlanta.

30. See "Snapshots," p. 14.

31. Morgan, "More Than The Three R's," p. 74.

32. "Annual Report of the Director," *Journal of Adult Education*, 5:1 (1944), p. 353.

33. Sinnette, *Arthur Alfonso Schomburg*, p. 171.

34. *Ibid.*

35. "Annual Report of the Director," p. 353.

36. Ira Reid, *Adult Education Among Negroes*, pp. 19–20.

37. See Locke Papers, Moorland-Spingarn Research Center, Washington, D.C.

38. Locke to Morse Cartwright, Locke Papers, Moorland-Spingarn Research Center, Washington, D.C.

39. Locke, "Report on Negro Adult Education Projects," Locke Papers, Moorland-Spingarn Research Center, Washington, D.C.

40. *Ibid.*

41. *Ibid.*

42. *Ibid.*

43. *Ibid.*

44. *Ibid.*

45. Alain Locke, "The Harlem Experiment," *Journal of Adult Education*, 5 (June 1933), p. 301.

46. Locke, "Report on Negro Adult Education Projects," Locke Papers, Moorland-Spingarn Research Center, Washington, D.C.

47. *Ibid.*

48. *Ibid.*

49. Alain Locke, "The Intellectual Interests of Negroes," *Journal of Adult Education*, 6 (1935-1936), p. 35.

50. Ira Reid, *Adult Education Among Negroes*, p. 25.

51. Letter from Rosenwald fund to Morse Cartwright, dated 12 June 1934, Locke Papers, Moorland-Spingarn Research Center, Washington, D.C.

52. Letter from Eugene Jones to Morse Cartwright, 15 May 1934, Locke Papers, Moorland-Spingarn Research Center, Washington, D.C.

53. Days, *Alain Leroy Locke*, p. 110.

54. See Organization's Minutes and Program Descriptions, Auburn Avenue Research Library on African American History and Culture, Atlanta.

55. Letter to Locke from Cartwright, 23 January 1935, Locke Papers, Moorland-Spingarn Research Center, Washington, D.C.

56. Sinnette, *Arthur Alfonso Schomburg*, p. 171.

57. See Editorial Statement in Bronze Booklets.

58. Alain Locke, "The Intellectual Interest of Negroes," *Journal of Adult Education*, 8:6 (1935-1936), p. 352. Also see original draft of speech among Locke Papers, Moorland-Spingarn Research Center, Washington, D.C.

59. *Ibid.*

60. *Ibid.*

61. Alain Locke, "Adult Education for Negroes," *Handbook of Adult Education,* ed. Malcolm Knowles, (New York: American Association for Adult Education, 1936), p. x.

62. See *Bronze Booklets.*

63. M. Anthony Fitchue, "Locke and DuBois: Two Major Black Voices Muzzled by Philanthropic Organizations," *The Journal of Higher Education* (Winter 1997), No. 4, p. 113.

64. Locke Papers, Moorland-Spingarn Research Center, Washington, D.C.

65. *Ibid.*

66. *Ibid.*

67. Margaret Just Butcher, *The Negro in America*: Based on materials left by Alain Leroy Locke (New York: Knopf, 1956), p. 38.

68. Eric Williams, *The Negro in the Caribbean* (Washington, D.C.: Associates in Negro Folk Education, 1942).

69. See "Table of Contents." In Alain Locke, *Negro Art: Past and Present* (Washington, D.C.: Associates in Negro Folk Education, 1936).

70. Leonard Harris, *The Philosophy of Alain Locke: Harlem Renaissance and Beyond* (Philadelphia: Temple University Press, 1987), p. 5.

71. *Ibid.*

72. Richard Long, "Alain Locke: Cultural and Social Mentor," *Black World*, 20 (1970), p. 89.

73. Alain Locke (ed.), *The New Negro* (New York: Antheneum, 1970, originally published in 1925), p. 12.

74. Eugene Holmes, "Alain Locke: Philosopher, Critic, Spokesman," *Journal of Philosophy*, 2I:5 (28 February 1957), p. 114. The original Speech was read at a Memorial for Alain Locke held at New York University, 29 October 1955.

75. Long, "Alain Locke: Cultural and Social Critic." p. 87.

76. *Ibid.,* p. 89.

77. Ralph Bunche, *World View of Race* (Washington, D.C.: Associates in Negro Folk Education, 1936), p. 75.

78. *Ibid.,* p. 28.

79. Jeffrey Stewart (ed.), *Alain Leroy Locke/Race Contacts and Interracial Relations* (Washington, D.C.: Howard University Press, 1992), p. xlvii.

80. Toni Morrison, *Playing in the Dark* (New York: Vintage Books, 1993), p. 12.

81. Long, "Alain Locke: Cultural and Social Critic," p. 89.

82. Carnegie Corporation Grant Files, Columbia University Library, New York.

83. Morse Cartwright to F. P. Keppel, 10 April 1989, Carnegie Corporation Grant Files, Columbia University Library.

84. *Ibid.*

85. Letter to Association Members, Locke Papers, Moorland-Spingarn Research Center, Washington, D.C.

86. Woodson to Locke, 4 April 1935, Locke Papers, Moorland-Spingarn Research Center, Washington, D.C.

87. Locke to Woodson, 8 April 1935, Locke Papers, Moorland-Spingarn Research Center, Washington, D.C.

88. Sinnette, *Arthur Alfonso Schomburg*, p. 172.

89. Russell J. Linnemann (ed.), *Alain Locke: Reflections on a Modern Renaissance Man* (Baton Rouge, La.: Louisiana State University, 1982), p. 71.

90. Locke to DuBois, 30 May 1936, In Herbert Aptheker, *Correspondence of W.E.B. DuBois* (Amherst, Mass.: University of Massachusetts, 1976), pp. 81–84.

91. Talmadge Carter Guy, "Prophecy from the Periphery: Alain Locke's Philosophy of Cultural Pluralism and Adult Education," (Ed.D dissertation, Northern Illinois University, DeKalb, 1993), pp. 163–165.

92. Locke letter to Bryson 8 June 1939, Locke Papers, Moorland-Spingarn Research Center, Washington, D.C.

93. Talmadge Guy, "The American Association of Adult Education and the Experiments in African American Adult Education." *Freedom Road: Adult Education of African Americans,* ed. Elizabeth A. Peterson, (Malabar, Fla.: Krieger Publishing Company, 1996), p. 102.

94. Fitchue, "Locke and DuBois," p. 114.

95. W.E.B. DuBois, "Dusk of Dawn," *An Essay Toward an Autobiography of a Race Concept* (New York: Harcourt Brace, 1940), pp. 320–321.

96. Locke, *The New Negro,* p. 4

97. See Amy Jacques Garvey (ed.), *Philosophy and Opinion of Marcus Garvey* (New York: Atheneum, 1992).

98. Alain Locke, "Negro Needs as Adult Education Opportunities," *The Philosophy of Alain Locke*, ed. Leonard Harris, p. 257. Also, see Locke Papers, Moorland-Spingarn Research Center, Washington, D.C.

99. *Ibid.*

100. Robert Hayden and Eugene DuBois, "A Drum Major for Black Adult Education: Alain Locke," *The Western Journal of Black Studies* (December 1977), p. 285.

101. Holmes, "Alain Locke and the Adult Education Movement," p. 7.

102. *Ibid.*, p. 10.

103. *Ibid.*

104. Linnemann, *Alain Locke: Reflections on a Modern Renaissance Man*, p. 106.

105. Alain Locke, *The Negro in Art: A Pictorial Record of the Negro Artist and of the Negro Themes in Art* (Washington, D.C.: Associates of Negro Folk Education, 1940), p. 178.

106. Sarah Fitzgerald, "The Homecoming of Jacob Lawrence," *American Vision,* April-May 1995, p. 24.

107. Tribota Haynes Benjamin, "Lois Mailou Jones," *American Vision*, (June-July) 1993, pp. 36–39.

108. Linnemann, *Alain Locke: Reflections*, p. xii.

109. Morse Cartwright to F. P. Keppel, 1 December 1938, Carnegie Corporation Grant Files, Series #1, Columbia University Library.

110. Alfred Barr to F. P. Keppel, 23 November 1938, Series #1, Columbia University Library.

111. Locke to F. P. Keppel, 20 December 1938, Carnegie Corporation Grant Files, Series #1, Columbia University Library.

112. *Ibid.*

113. Alain Locke, *The Negro in Art: A Pictorial Record of the Negro Artist and of the Negro Themes in Art* (Washington, D.C.: Associates in Negro Folk Education, 1940).

114. *Ibid.*

115. Fitchue, "Locke and DuBois," p. 112.

116. Days, "Alain Locke," p. 112.

117. *Findings of the First Annual Conference on Adult Education and the Negro* (Hampton, Va.: Hampton Institute Press, 1938), p. 3.

118. Days, "Alain Locke," pp. 112–113.

119. *Findings of the First Annual Conference on Adult Education and the Negro,* p. 5.

120. *Ibid.*

121. Alain Locke, "Negro Needs as Adult Education Opportunities," rough draft, 20 October 1938, Locke Papers, Moorland-Spingarn Research Center, Washington, D.C, pp. 5–6. Also, see Leonard Harris, *The Philosophy of Alain Locke,* pp. 253–262.

122. *Findings of The First Annual Conference on Adult Education and the Negro.*

123. *Ibid.*

124. Guy, "Prophesy," pp. 176–177.

125. See *Findings of the Second Annual Conference on Adult Education and the Negro* (Tuskegee: Tuskegee Institute Press, 1940).

126. *Ibid.*

127. Days, "Alain Locke." Also, see Locke "Popularized Literature" in *Findings of the Second Annual Conference on Adult Education and the Negro*, p. 50.

128. See *Findings of Second Annual on Adult Education and the Negro*, p. 49.

129. Locke, "Education for Adulthood," *Adult Education Journal*, 6 (July 1947), p. 74.

130. Days, "Alain Locke (1886-1954): Pioneer in Adult Education and a Catalyst in the Adult Education Movement for Black Americans," p. 125.

131. L.D. Riddick, "Adult Education and the Improvement of Race Relations," *Journal of Adult Education*, 14 (Summer 1945), p. 191.

132. *Findings of the Second Annual Conference on Adult Education and the Negro.*

133. *Findings of the Third Annual Conference on Adult Education and the Negro.*

134. Days, "Alain Leroy Locke," p. 127. Also see *Findings of the Third Annual Conference.*

135. Days, "Alain Leroy Locke (1886-1954): Pioneer in Adult Education and a Catalyst in the Adult Education Movement for Black Americans," pp. 127–130.

136. Neufeldt and McGee, p. 129. Also see *Findings of the Fourth Annual Conference on Adult Education and the Negro* (Atlanta: Atlanta University Press, 1942), pp. 60–61, 63–71.

137. Guy, *Prophesy*, pp. 168–169.

138. Alain Locke, "Areas of Extension and Improvement of Adult Education Among Negroes," *Journal of Negro Education*, 14 (1945), p. 453.

139. *Ibid.*

140. Alain Locke, "Coming of Age," *Adult Education Journal*, 6 (January 1947), p. 3.

141. *Ibid.*, pp. 2–3.

142. Letter to Locke from Cartwright, 10 May 1946, Locke Papers, Moorland-Spingarn Research Center, Washington, D.C.

143. Mary Ely to Locke, 10 May 1946, Locke Papers, Moorland-Spingarn Research Center, Washington, D.C.

144. Frederick Hall to Locke, 4 May 1946, Locke Papers, Moorland-Spingarn Research Center, Washington, D.C.

145. Alain Locke, "Education for Adulthood," *Adult Education Journal*, 6 (July 1947), p. 104.

146. See Mayor Fiorello LaGuardia Papers, New York Municipal Archives.

147. Alain Locke, "Harlem: Dark Weathervane," *Survey Graphic,* 24 (August 1936), p. 493.

Chapter Four

1. Booker T. Washington, *Up From Slavery* (New York: Gramercy Books, 1993, p. 205, reprint, originally published in 1901).

2. W.E.B. DuBois, *The Souls of Black Folk* (New York: Gramercy Books, 1994, p. 73, reprint, originally published in 1903).

3. Margaret Just Butcher, *The Negro in American Culture, Based on Materials Left by Alain Locke.* (New York: Alfred A. Knopf, 1957), p. 17.

4. Frederick Dunn, "The Educational Philosophies of Washington, DuBois and Houston: Laying the Foundation for Afro-Centrism and Multi-Culturalism," *The Journal of Negro Education,* 62:1 (Winter 1993), p. 25.

5. Booker T. Washington, *Up From Slavery* (New York: Lancer Books, Inc., 1968), pp. 217–236.

6. See Johnny Washington, *Alain Locke and Philosophy: A Quest for Cultural Pluralism* (New York: Greenwood Press, 1986), pp. 144–145.

7. *Ibid.*, p. 143.

8. Haywood Burns, "The Washington-DuBois Controversy," *Afro-American Studies* (1970), p. 55.

9. Washington, *Up From Slavery* (1968), 7th edition, p. 223.

10. W.E.B. DuBois, *The Souls of Black Folk* (Greenwich: Fawcett Publications, 1961).

11. Virginia Lantz Denton, *Booker T. Washington and the Adult Education Movement* (Tallahassee: Board of Regents of the State of Florida, 1993), p. 153.

12. DuBois, *The Souls of Black Folk*, pp. 53–54.

13. Burns, "The Washington-Dubois Controversy," p. 54. Also see original in W.E.B. DuBois, *Dusk at Dawn* (New York: Harcourt, Brace and Company, Inc., 1940).

14. Alain Locke, "Negro Needs as Adult Education Opportunities," p. 6. in *Findings of the First Annual Conference on Adult Education and the Negro* (Hampton, Va.: Hampton Institute Press, 1935. Also, see *The Philosophy of Alain Locke: Harlem Renaissance and Beyond,* ed. Leonard Harris. (Philadelphia: Temple University Press, 1989), pp. 253–261.

15. Johnny Washington, *Alain Locke and Philosophy*, p. 132.

16. Burns, "The Washington-DuBois Controversy," p. 56.

17. Marable Manning, *W.E.B. DuBois: Black Radical Democrat* (Boston: Twayne Publishers, 1986), p. 51.

18. Booker T. Washington, *Up From Slavery*, 11th edition, p. 220.

19. *Ibid.,* p. 223.

20. James E. Jackson, "W.E.B. DuBois: Light for the Path," *Political Affairs* (July 1989), p. 3.

21. Booker T. Washington, *Up From Slavery* (1968), 7th edition, p. 123.

22. Harold Cruse, *Plural but Unequal: A Critical Study of Blacks and Minorities and America's Plural Society* (New York: Quill, William, Morrow, 1987), p. 2.

23. Alain Locke. "Negro Education Bids for Par," *Survey 54* (1 September 1945), p. 569. Also, see Alain Locke "Negro Education Bids Par," *The Philosophy of Alain Locke*, ed. Leonard Harris, p. 245.

24. Alain Locke, *The Negro in America* (Chicago: American Library Association, 1933), p. 29.

25. Johnny Washington, *Alain Locke and Philosophy*, p. 149.

26. *Ibid.*

27. Locke, "Negro Needs as Adult Education Opportunities," p. 257.

28. Johnny Washington, *Alain Locke and Philosophy* (Westport, Ct.: Greenwood Press, 1986), p. 34. Also see Johnny Washington, "Alain Locke's Values and Imperatives: An Interpretation," *Philosophy Born of Struggle* ed. Leonard Harris, (Dubuque, Iowa: Kendall-Hunt, 1983), pp. 148–158.

29. DuBois, *The Souls of Black Folk,* p. 42.

30. Johnny Washington, *Alain Locke and Philosophy*, pp. 12–15.

31. *Ibid.*

32. Philip Foner, *W.E.B. DuBois – Speeches and Addresses*, 1920-1963 (New York: Pathfinder, 1970), p. 132.

33. Locke, "Negro Education Bids," p. 250.

34. W.E.B. DuBois, "The Talented Tenth Memorial Address," *Boule Journal*, 15 (1948), p. 5. Also, see Francis L. Broderick and August Meir (eds.), *Negro Protest Thought in the Twentieth Century.* (Indianapolis: Bobbs-Merrill Company, 1965), p. 4.

35. James Stewart, "The Legacy of W.E.B. DuBois for Contemporary Black Studies," *The Journal of Negro Education*, 8:3 (1984), p. 306.

36. Johnny Washington, *Alain Locke and Philosophy*, p. 136.

37. W.E.B. DuBois, "The Talented Tenth," in Henry Louis Gates, Jr., and Cornel West, *The Future of the Race* (New York: Alfred A. Knopf, 1996), p. 133. First published in W.E.B. DuBois, *The Negro Problem*, 1903.

38. Alain Locke, "The Role of the Talented Tenth," *Howard University Record*, vol. 12, p. 15.

39. Everette Alston Days, "Alain Leroy Locke (1886-1954): Pioneer in Adult Education and Catalyst in the Adult Education Movement for Black Americans." (Ed.D., dissertation, North Carolina State University at Raleigh, 1978.

40. Alain Locke, "Negro Needs as Adult Education Opportunities," *Findings of the First Conference on Adult Education and the Negro* (Hampton: Hampton Institute, 1938), p. 6.

41. Johnny Washington, *Alain Locke and Philosophy*, p. 149.

42. Burns, "The Washington-Dubois Controversy," p. 59.

43. Harold Cruse, *The Crisis of the Negro Intellectual* (New York: Quill, 1984), p. 176.

44. DuBois, *The Souls of Black Folk*, pp. 51–52.

45. Alain Locke, "Values and Imperatives," in Horace M. Kallen and Sidney Hook (eds), *American Philosophy, Today and Tomorrow* (New York: Lee Furman, 1935), p. 328. Also, see Ernest D. Mason, "Alain Locke's Philosophy of Value," ed., Russell J. Linnemann, *Alain Locke: Reflections on a Modern Renaissance* (Baton Rouge, La.: Louisiana State University, 1932), p. 46.

46. Johnny Washington, *Alain Locke and Philosophy*, p. 144.

47. Locke, "Values and Imperatives," p. 328.

48. Johnny Washington, *Alain Locke and Philosophy*, pp. 78–79.

49. Burns, "The Washington-DuBois Controversy," p. 59.

50. David Levering Lewis, *W.E.B DuBois: Biography of Race* (New York: Henry Holt and Company, 1993), p. 502.

51. Denton, *Booker T. Washington and the Adult Education Movement*, p. 199.

52. Johnny Washington, *Alain Locke and Philosophy*, p. 132.

53. Burns, "The Washington-DuBois Controversy," p. 56.

54. *Ibid.*

55. Lewis, *W.E.B. DuBois*, pp. 150–151.

56. Denton, *Booker T. Washington and the Adult Education Movement*, p. 159.

57. Burns, "The Washington-DuBois Controversy," p. 56.

58. Butcher, *The Negro in American Culture*, pp. 9–10.

Chapter Five

1. Malcolm X, "Message to the Grassroots." Speech given in Detroit, Michigan, 10 November 1963.

2. Alain Locke, "Whiter Race Relations: A Critical Commentary," *Journal of Negro Education,* 13:3 (Summer 1944), p. 398.

3. Alain Locke, "What Adults Want to Learn," Locke Papers, Moorland-Spingarn Research Center, Washington, D.C., p. 8.

4. Johnny Washington, *Alain Locke and Philosophy: A Quest for Cultural Pluralism* (New York: Greenwood Press, 1986), pp. 157–158

5. Alain Locke, "Commencement Address: Fisk University," 19 June 1937, Locke Papers, Moorland-Spingarn Research Center, New York, p. 1.

6. Alain Locke, "Negro Need as Adult Education Opportunities," speech delivered at the First Annual Conference. See Locke Papers, Moorland-Spingarn Research Center. Also catalogued at the Schomburg Center for Research in Black Culture under "Findings of the First Annual Conference on Adult Education and the Negro." Also included in Leonard Harris, *The Philosophy of Alain Locke: Harlem Renaissance and Beyond* (Philadelphia: Temple University, 1989), pp. 225–261.

7. Douglass K. Stafford, "Alain Locke: The Child, the Man, and the People," *The Journal of Negro Education,* 30 (1961), p. 34.

8. Charlotte Morgan, "More than the Three R's: The Development of Black Adult Education in Manhattan." *Adult Education in Multi-Cultural Society,* ed. Beverly Cassera, (New York: Routledge, 1990), p. 69.

9. Locke, "What Adults Want to Learn," p. 8.

10. Mavlana Karenga, *The African American Holiday of Kwanzaa: A Celebration of Family, Community, and Culture* (Los Angeles: University of Sankora Press, 1988.

11. Margaret Just Butcher, *The Negro in American Culture: Based on Materials Left by Alain Leroy Locke* (New York: Alfred A. Knopf, 1956), p. 7.

12. Alain Locke, "A Concrete Suggestion: In Confidential Memo to Mayor LaGuardia from Alain Locke, Regarding Harlem Commission Report" (12 June 1936), LaGuardia papers, New York Municipal Archives, p. 5.

13. Locke, "What Adults Want to Learn," p. 10.

14. Alain Locke, "Lessons of Negro Adult Education," in M.L. Ely (ed.), *Adult Education in Action* (New York: American Association for Adult Education, 1936), p. 226.

15. Locke, "Whiter Race Relations: A Critical Commentary."

16. Russell J. Linnemann (ed.), *Alain Locke: Reflections on a Modern Renaissance Man* (Baton Rouge, La.: Louisiana State University, 1982).

17. Molefi Kete Asante, "The Africentric Idea in Education," *The Journal of Negro Education*, 60:2 (1991), p. 171.

18. Greg Thomas, "The Black Studies: Multiculturalism versus Afrocentricity," *Voice* (17 January 1995), p. 29.

19. *Ibid.*, p. 27.

20. William Cross, *Shades of Black* (Philadelphia: Temple University Press, 1991), p. 189.

21. Linnemann, *Alain Locke: Reflections.*

22. Johnny Washington, *Alain Locke and Philosophy*, p. 125.

23. Cornel West and bell hooks, *Breaking Bread: Insurgent Black Intellectual Life* (Boston: South End Press, 1991), p. 29.

24. Butcher, *The Negro in American Culture*, p. xi.

ABOUT THE AUTHOR

Rudolph Alexander Kofi Cain, who shares the same birthday/earthday with Alain Leroy Locke, is Professor of Education and mentor at State University of New York, Empire State College, where he is also the Director of the Bedford-Stuyvesant Unit. He teaches in the areas of Educational Studies and Community and Human Services, and his interests extend to Africana Studies and Adult Development and Aging. He has thirty years experience of counseling, teaching, and administrative service, having had prior academic affiliations with Pace University and Medgar Evers College of the City University of New York. His scholarly publications have appeared in such professional/trade journals as *Black Issues in Higher Education, The Journal of Negro Education, The Journal of Continuing Higher Education, The Western Journal of Black Studies*, and *The Educational Forum*. He received his doctorate in Adult Education from Teachers College, Columbia University, with a secondary specialization in Psychology. His Master of Science degree in Rehabilitation Counseling was received from New York University. Hampton Institute, currently Hampton University, awarded his baccalaureate degree in psychology and sociology.

Arthur Schomburg

Adult Education Activity, Harlem Experiment in Negro Adult Education

Adult Education Activity, Atlanta Experiment in Negro Adult Education

W.E.B. DuBois at Desk

W.E.B. DuBois (center) with Mary McLeod Bethune (left),
and Horace Mann Bond (right)

Booker T. Washington

Booker T. Washington (seated third from left),
His Wife, Benefactors, and Faculty

BIBLIOGRAPHY

Aptheker, Herbert. *Correspondence of W.E.B. DuBois.* Amherst: University of Massachusetts Press, 1976.

Asante, Molefi. *Kemet: Afrocentricity and Knowledge.* Trenton, N.J.: African World Press, 1990.

————. "The Africentric Idea in Education," *The Journal of Negro Education,* 60:2 (1991), pp. 170–180.

Adkins, James A. "Special Training Needed by Adult Education and the Negro," *Findings of the Second Annual Conference on Adult Education and the Negro.* Tuskegee: Tuskegee Institute, 1940, pp. 29–36.

Belles, A. Gilbert "The Politics of Alain Locke," *Alain Locke: Reflections on a Modern Renaissance Man.* Edited by Russell J. Linnemann. Baton Rouge, La.: Louisiana State University, 1992, pp. 50–62.

Benjamin, Trioba Haynes. "Lois Mailou Jones," *American Vision* (June-July 1993), pp. 36–39.

Broderick, Francis L. and Meir, August (eds.). *Negro Protest Thought in the Twentieth Century.* Indianapolis: Bobbs-Merrill Company, 1965.

Brown, Sterling. *The Negro in American Fiction.* Washington, D.C.: Associates in Negro Folk Education, 1937.

————. *The Negro in Poetry and Drama.* Washington, D.C.: Associates in Negro Folk Education, 1937.

Bryson, Lyman. *Adult Education.* New York: America Book Company, 1936.

Bunche, Ralph. *World View of Race.* Washington, D.C.: Associates in Negro Folk Education, 1936.

Burgett, David Joseph. "Vindication as a Thematic Principle in Alain Locke's Writings on the Music of African Americans," *The Harlem Renaissance: Revaluations.* Edited by A. Singh, W. Shriver, and S. Brodwin. New York: Garland Publishing, Inc., 1989, pp. 140–141.

Burns, Haywood. "The Washington-DuBois Controversy," *Afro-American Studies,* 1 (1970), pp. 55–62.

Butcher, Margaret. *The Negro in American Culture: Based on Materials Left by Alain Leroy Locke.* New York: Knopf, 1956.

Cassaria, Betty (ed.). *Adult Education in a Multi-Cultural Society.* London: Routledge, 1990.

Cross, William. *Shades of Black.* Philadelphia: Temple University Press, 1991.

Cruse, Harold. *The Crisis of the Negro Intellectual.* New York: Quill, 1984.

————. *Plural But Unequal: A Critical Study of Blacks and Minorities and America's Plural Society.* New York: Quill/William Morrow, 1987.

Days, Everett, A. "Alain Leroy Locke (1886-1954): Pioneer in Adult Education and a Catalyst in the Adult Education Movement For African Americans," Ed.D. dissertation. North Carolina University at Raleigh, 1978.

Denton, Virginia Lantz. *Booker T. Washington and the Adult Education Movement.* Tallahassee, Fla.: Board of Regents of the State of Florida, 1933.

DuBois, W.E.B. "The Talented Tenth," *The Future of Race.* Edited by Henry Louis Gates, Jr. and Cornel West. New York: Alfred A. Knopf, 1986, pp. 133–157.

————. "Dusk at Dawn," *Dusk at Dawn: An Essay Toward an Autobiography of a Race Concept.* New York: Harcourt Brace, 1940, pp. 312–326.

————. *The Souls of Black Folk.* New York: Gramercy Books, 1994, 1903 reprint.

————. "The Talented Tenth," *Boule Journal,* 15 (1948), pp. 5–9.

Dunn, Frederick. "The Educational Philosophies of Washington, DuBois, and Houston: Laying the Foundation for Afro-Centrism and Multi-Culturalism," *Journal in Higher Education,* 62:1 (Winter, 1993), pp. 25–34.

Findings of the First Annual Conference on Adult Education and the Negro. Hampton, Va.: Hampton Institute Press, 1938.

Findings of the Fourth Annual Conference on Adult Education and the Negro. Atlanta: Atlanta University Press, 1942.

Findings of the Second Annual Conference on Adult Education and the Negro. Tuskegee: Tuskegee Institute, 1940.

Findings of the Third Annual Conference on Adult Education and the Negro. Washington, D.C.: Howard University Press, 1941.

Fitchue, Anthony M. "Locke and DuBois: Two Major Black Voices Muzzled by Philanthropic Organizations," *Journal in Higher Education,* 4 (Winter, 1996-1997), pp. 112–115.

Fitzgerald, Sarah. "The Homecoming of Jacob Lawrence," *American Vision* (April-May 1995), pp. 24–26.

Foner, Phillip. *W.E.B. DuBois Speaks: Speeches and Addresses, 1890-1919.* New York: Pathfinder, 1970.

Freire, Paulo. *Pedagogy of the Oppressed.* New York: Continuum, 1970.

―――――. *Educating for Critical Consciousness.* New York: Continuum, 1973.

Gardner, Howard. *Multiple Intelligences.* New York: Basic Books, 1993.

Garvey, Amy Jacques (ed.). *Philosophy and Opinions of Marcus Garvey.* New York: Atheneum, 1992.

Gleason, Eliza. *The Southern Negro and the Library.* Chicago: University of Chicago Press, 1941.

Gyant, La Verne. "Contributions to Adult Education: Booker T. Washington, George Washington Carver, Alain Locke, and Ambrose Caliver," *Journal of Black Studies,* 19:1 (September 1988), pp. 97–109.

Guy, Talmadge C. "The American Association of Adult Education and the Experiments in African American Education," *Freedom Road-Adult Education of African Americans.* Edited by Elizabeth Peterson. Malabar, Fla.: Krieger Publishing Company, 1996, pp. 101–104.

―――――. "Prophesy from the Periphery: Alain Locke's Philosophy of Cultural Pluralism and Adult Education," Ed.D. dissertation. Northern Illinois University at DeKalb, 1993.

Harris, Leonard (ed.). *The Philosophy Born of Struggle.* Dubuque, Iowa: Kendall Press, 1987.

―――――. *The Philosophy of Alain Locke-Harlem Renaissance and Beyond.* Philadelphia: Temple University Press, 1989.

Hawes, Mae. "Snapshots of the Atlanta Experiment in Adult Education Among Negroes," October 1931-August 1932, Annie L. McPheeter's Collection/Auburn Avenue Research Library on African American Culture and History. Atlanta: 1933.

Hayden, Robert and DuBois, Eugene. "A Drum Major for Black Adult Education: Alain Locke," *The Western Journal of Black Studies,* 1:4 (December 1977), pp. 293–296.

Helbling, Mark. "Alain Locke: Ambivalence and Hope," *Phylon,* 40:3 (1979), pp. 291–300.

Hill, Arnold T. *The Negro and Economic Reconstruction.* Washington, D.C.: Associates in Negro Folk Education, 1937.

Holmes, Eugene. "Alain Locke: Philosopher, Critic, and Spokesman," *The Journal of Philosophy,* 54:5 (28 February 1957), pp. 113–120.

————. "The Legacy of Alain Locke," *Freedomways,* 3:3 (1963), pp. 306–310.

————. "Alain Locke and the Adult Education Movement," *Journal of Negro Education,* 34:1 (1965), pp. 5–10.

Jackson, James E. "W.E.B. DuBois: Light for the Path," *Political Affairs* (July 1989), pp. 3–4.

Kallen, Horace. "Locke and Cultural Pluralism," *The Journal of Philosophy,* 54:5 (28 February 1957), pp. 123–126.

Karenga, Maulana. *The African American Holiday of Kwanzaa: A Celebration of Family, Community & Culture.* Los Angeles: University of Sankora Press, 1988.

Knowles, Malcolm. *A History of Adult Education in the United States.* Malabar, Fla: Kreiger Publishing Company, 1977.

————. *Applying Modern Principles of Adult Learning.* San Francisco: Malcolm S. Knowles Associates, 1984.

————. *The Modern Practice of Adult Education: From Pedagogy to Andragogy.* Chicago: Association Press, 1980, revised.

Lewis, David Levering. *W.E.B. DuBois: Biography of Race.* New York: Henry Holt and Company, 1993.

————. *When Harlem Was in Vogue.* New York: Oxford University Press, 1981.

Lindeman, Eduard C. *The Meaning of Adult Education.* Montreal: Harvest House, 1961. 1926 Reprint.

Linnemann, Russell J. (ed.). *Alain Locke: Reflections on a Modern Renaissance Man.* Baton Rouge, La.: Louisiana State University, 1982.

Locke, Alain Leroy. "Adult Education for Negroes," *Handbook of Adult Education.* Edited by Malcolm S. Knowles. New York: American Association for Adult Education, 1936, pp. 25–26.

————. "Adult Education: Safeguard and Democracy." Speech delivered at the Southeastern Regional Conference of the American Association for Adult Education (undated), Locke Papers, Moorland-Spingarn Research Center, Howard University, Washington, D.C.

————. "Areas of Extension and Improvement of Adult Education," *Journal of Negro Education,* 14 (1945), pp. 453–459.

————. "Coming of Age," *Adult Education Journal,* 6:1 (January 1947), pp. 1–3.

————. "Commencement Address: Fisk University," (19 June 1937), Locke Papers, Moorland-Spingarn Research Center, Howard University, Washington, D.C.

————. "A Concrete Suggestion: In Confidential Memo to LaGuardia from Alain Locke, Regarding Harlem Commission Report," (2 June 1936), LaGuardia Papers/ New York Municipal Archives, New York.

————. "Cultural Relativism and Ideological Power," *The Philosophy of Alain Locke: Harlem Renaissance and Beyond.* Edited by Leonard Harris. Philadelphia: Temple University Press, 1989, pp. 67–78.

————. "Education for Adulthood," *Adult Education Journal,* 5 (July 1947), pp. 104–111.

————. "Enter the New Negro," *Survey Graphic,* 53 (1925), pp. 633–637.

————. "Frontiers of Culture," The Crescent: Official Organ of the Phi Beta Sigma Fraternity, 33:1 (1950), p.37.

————. "Harlem: Dark Weathervane," *Survey Graphic,* 24 (August 1936), p. 493.

————. "Intellectual Interests of Negroes," *Journal of Adult Education,* 12 (1935), pp. 352–357.

————. "Lessons of Negro Adult Education," *Adult Education in Action.* Edited by M. L. Ely. New York: American Association for Adult Education, 1935.

————. "Minorities and the Social Mind," *Progressive Education,* 12 (1935), pp. 141–146.

————. "The Need for a New Organon in Education: Goals for American Education," *Proceedings of the Ninth Conference on Science, Philosophy and Relgion.* New York: Conference on Science Philosophy and Religion, 1950, pp. 201–212.

————. *The Negro in Art: A Pictorial Record of the Negro Artist and of the Negro Theme in Art.* Washington, D.C.: Associates for Negro Folk Education, 1940.

————. *The Negro and Art: Past and Present.* Washington, D.C.: Associates for Negro Folk Education, 1936.

————. *The Negro and His Music* Washington, D.C.: Associates for Negro Folk Education, 1936.

————. "Negro Education Bids Par," *Survey Graphic,* 24 (August 1936), pp. 567–570.

————. *The Negro in America.* Chicago: American Library Association, 1933.

————. "The Negro Needs as Adult Education Opportunities," *Findings of the First Annual Conference on Adult Education and the Negro.* Hampton, Va.: Hampton Institute, 1938.

————. "Negro Needs Adult Education," *The Philosophy of Alain Locke: Harlem Renaissance and Beyond.* Edited by Leonard Harris. Philadelphia: Temple University Press, 1984, pp. 253–261

————. *The New Negro: An Interpretation.* New York: Albert and Charles Boni, 1925.

————. "Pluralism and Ideological Peace," *Freedom and Experience.* Edited by Milton Konvitz and Sidney Hook. Ithaca, N.Y.: Cornell University Press, 1947.

————. "Popularized Literature," in *Findings of the Second Annual Conference on Adult Education and the Negro.* Tuskegee, Ala.: Tuskegee Institute, 1940.

————. "Report on Negro Adult Education Projects," Locke Papers, Moorland-Spingarn Research Center, Howard University, Washington, D.C.

————. "The Role of the Talented Tenth," *Howard University Record*, 12:8 (December 1948), pp. 15–18.

————. "Trends in Adult Education for Negroes," Locke Papers, Moorland-Spingarn Research Center, Howard University, Washington, D.C.

————. "Values and Imperatives," *American Philosophy, Today and Tomorrow.* Edited by Horace Kallen and Sidney Hook. New York: Lee Furman, 1935.

————. " Values that Matter," *Key Reporter,* 19 (May 1954), p. 54.

Logan, Rayford W. and Winston, Michael R. (eds.). *The Dictionary of American Negro Biography.* New York: Norton, 1983.

Long, Huey. *New Perspectives on the Education of Adults in the United States.* London: Croom Helm, 1987.

Long, Richard. "Alain Locke: Cultural and Social Critic," *Black World,* 20 (1970), pp. 87–90.

Mason, Ernest. "Alain Locke's Philosophy of Value," *Alain Locke: Reflections on a Modern Renaissance Man.* Edited by Russell Linnemann. Baton Rouge, La.: Louisiana State University, 1982, pp. 1–16.

Morgan, Charlotte. "More than the Three R's: The Development of Black Adult Education," *Manhattan Adult Education in a Multi-Cultural Society.* Edited by Beverly Cassaria. New York: Routledge, 1990, pp. 63–77.

Morrison, Toni. *Playing in the Dark.* New York: Vintage Books, 1993.

Neufeldt, Harvey G. and McGee, Leo (eds.). *Education of the African American Adult.* New York: Greenwood Press, 1990.

Peterson, Elizabeth (ed.). *Freedom Road: Adult Education of African Americans.* Malabar, Fla.: Kreiger Publishing Company, 1996.

Reid, Ira. *Adult Education among Negroes.* Washington, D.C.: Associates in Negro Folk Education, 1936.

Reid, Sara E. "Harlem Adult Education." Speech delivered at the National Conference on Fundamental Problems in the Education of Negroes, 9-12 May 1934, Washington, D.C.

Riddick, L. D. "Adult Education and the Improvement of Race Relations," *Journal of Negro Education,* 14:3 (Summer 1945), pp. 488–493.

Rose, Ernestine. "Report of Harlem Adult Education Experiment to Mr. Cartwright for the Year 1932," Countee Cullen Library Collection/Schomburg Center for Research in Black Culture, Box 2, New York.

Sinnette , Des Verney Elinor. *Arthur Alfonso Schomburg: Black Bibliophile & Collector.* New York: New York Public Library and Detroit: Wayne State University Press, 1989.

Stafford, Douglass K. "Alain Locke: The Child, the Man, and the People," *Journal of Negro Education,* 30 (1961), pp. 25–34.

Stewart, James. "The Legacy of W.E.B. DuBois for Contemporary Black Studies," *The Journal of Negro Education,* 53:3 (1984), pp. 296–311.

Stewart, Jeffrey (ed.). *Alain Leroy Locke: Race Contacts and Interracial Relations.* Washington, D.C.: Howard University Press, 1992.

Stubblefield, Harold. *Towards a History of Adult Education in America: The Search for a Unifying Principle.* London: Croom Helm, 1988.

Thomas, Greg. "Black Studies: Multiculturalism versus Afrocentricity," *Voice* (17 January 1995), p. 29.

Townsend, William. "Toward Full Equality," *Adult Education Journal,* 5 (October 1946), pp. 105–106.

Washington, Booker T. *Up From Slavery.* New York: Grammercy Books, 1993, 1901 Reprint.

————. *Up From Slavery.* New York: Lancer Books, Inc., 1968, 1901 Reprint.

Washington, Johnny. *Alain Locke and Philosophy: A Quest for Cultural Pluralism.* New York: Greenwood Press, 1976.

————. *A Journey into the Philosophy of Alain Locke.* Westport, Ct.: Greenwood Press, 1994.

Watson, Steven. *The Harlem Renaissance.* New York: Pantheon Books, 1995.

West, Cornel and hooks, bell. *Breaking Bread.* Boston: South End Press, 1991.

Williams, Eric. *The Negro in the Caribbean.* Washington, D.C.: Associates in Negro Folk Education, 1942.

INDEX

abolitionists, 76
absolutism, 28, 30
Abyssinian Church, 42
Adult Education, 21–28
Adult Education Association, 25
Adult Education Among Negroes, (Reid)
    46, 49, 63–65, 67, 105–107, 110
Adult educationists, 32, 40, 44
Advisory Committee of the Harlem
    Experiment, 17
aesthetics, 89
African American Art, 3, 17, 43, 47–49,
    52, 59–60, 62, 98
African Americans, xiii, xv–xvi, xix, 1–
    5, 8–12, 14–17, 22–25, 27–30, 32–
    33, 35–37, 40, 43, 47–52, 54–55,
    58–59, 62–63, 65–66, 70, 73–75,
    77–79, 82–83, 85, 90, 92–99, 101–
    102, 105–110, 112–113
African Art, 47–48, 59, 62, 89
African Union Society of Oxford, 89
Africentric, 17
Alain Locke Philosophical Society, 99
American Association for Adult
    Education, 5–7, 16–17, 29, 32–33,
    36–37, 41, 44–45, 53–54, 59–60,
    63, 65, 68–71, 104–105, 107, 113
American Council on African Education/
    Committees on International
    Education and Cultural Relations,
    89
American Library Association, 31, 111
American Negro Academy, 89
American Society for Race Tolerance, 89
Americanization program, 23
Andragogues, 21, 104
andragogy, 21,–22, 95, 104
arbiter, 73, 82
Arendt, Hannah, 4
Armenia Conference, 83
"aristocracy of talent," 81
Aristotle, xix
Asante, Molefi, 17, 97–98

Associates in Negro Folk Education, 43–
    45, 53, 58, 63, 106, 108–109
Association for the Study of Negro Life
    and History, 53
Atkins, James, 27
Atlanta, 18, 32–33, 35–43, 49, 68, 77,
    81, 86, 98, 106, 110
Atlanta Experiment, 18, 33, 35–36, 98,
    106
Atlanta University, 43, 49, 63, 68, 110
Atlantic Exposition Speech, 73
Auburn Avenue Research Library on
    African American History and
    Culture, xix–xx, 106–107
axiology, 10, 12, 79, 82, 92–93

Bahai, 3, 47
Baltimore Museum of Art, 60
Barr, Alfred, 60, 109
Basic American Negro Creed, The, 55–
    56
Bearden, Romare, 62
Belle, A. Gilbert, 8, 102
Benin, 48
Benjamin, Tribota, 60, 109
ben-Jochannan, Yosef, 98
Bethune, Mary McLeod, 43, 63, 121
Bible, 12, 46, 59
Black Colleges, 92
Black Community, 76, 79, 81, 85
Black English, 90
Black Middle Class, 90
Boxill, Bernard, xix
Brathwaite, William, 18
Britain, 52
Broderick, Francis L., 112
Bronze Booklets, xiii, xv–xvi, xix–xx,
    4–6, 9–11, 13, 18, 22, 24, 31–32,
    35, 39, 43, 45, 49, 52, 54–55, 58–
    59, 73–74, 79–83, 90, 97, 99, 102–
    103, 108–109, 112–114
Bryson, Lyman, 54, 63, 67

VIBS

The **Value Inquiry Book Series** is co-sponsored by:

Titles Published

1. Noel Balzer, *The Human Being as a Logical Thinker*

2. Archie J. Bahm, *Axiology: The Science of Values*

3. H. P. P. (Hennie) Lötter, *Justice for an Unjust Society*

4. H. G. Callaway, *Context for Meaning and Analysis: A Critical Study in the Philosophy of Language*

5. Benjamin S. Llamzon, *A Humane Case for Moral Intuition*

6. James R. Watson, *Between Auschwitz and Tradition: Postmodern Reflections on the Task of Thinking.* A volume in **Holocaust and Genocide Studies**

7. Robert S. Hartman, *Freedom to Live: The Robert Hartman Story, edited by Arthur R. Ellis.* A volume in **Hartman Institute Axiology Studies**

8. Archie J. Bahm, *Ethics: The Science of Oughtness*

9. George David Miller, *An Idiosyncratic Ethics; Or, the Lauramachean Ethics*

10. Joseph P. DeMarco, *A Coherence Theory in Ethics*

11. Frank G. Forrest, *Valuemetrics: The Science of Personal and Professional Ethics.* A volume in **Hartman Institute Axiology Studies**

12. William Gerber, *The Meaning of Life: Insights of the World's Great Thinkers*

13. Richard T. Hull, Editor, *A Quarter Century of Value Inquiry: Presidential Addresses of the American Society for Value Inquiry.* A volume in **Histories and Addresses of Philosophical Societies**

14. William Gerber, *Nuggets of Wisdom from Great Jewish Thinkers: From Biblical Times to the Present*

15. Sidney Axinn, *The Logic of Hope: Extensions of Kant's View of Religion*

16. Messay Kebede, *Meaning and Development*

17. Amihud Gilead, *The Platonic Odyssey: A Philosophical-Literary Inquiry*

into the Phaedo

46.   Peter A. Redpath, Wisdom's Odyssey: From Philosophy to Transcendental *Sophistry*. A volume in **Studies in the History of Western Philosophy**

47.   Albert A. Anderson, *Universal Justice: A Dialectical Approach.* A volume in **Universal Justice**

48.   Pio Colonnello, *The Philosophy of José Gaos.* Translated from Italian by Peter Cocozzella. Edited by Myra Moss. Introduction by Giovanni Gullace. A volume in **Values in Italian Philosophy**

49.   Laura Duhan Kaplan and Laurence F. Bove, Editors, *Philosophical Perspectives on Power and Domination: Theories and Practices.* A volume in **Philosophy of Peace**

50.   Gregory F. Mellema, *Collective Responsibility*

51.   Josef Seifert, *What Is Life? The Originality, Irreducibility, and Value of Life.* A volume in **Central-European Value Studies**

52.   William Gerber, *Anatomy of What We Value Most*

53.   Armando Molina, *Our Ways: Values and Character*, Edited by Rem B. Edwards. A volume in **Hartman Institute Axiology Studies**

54.   Kathleen J. Wininger, *Nietzsche's Reclamation of Philosophy.* A volume in **Central-European Value Studies**

55.   Thomas Magnell, Editor, *Explorations of Value*

56.   HPP (Hennie) Lötter, *Injustice, Violence, and Peace: The Case of South Africa.* A volume in **Philosophy of Peace**

57.   Lennart Nordenfelt, *Talking About Health: A Philosophical Dialogue.* A volume in **Nordic Value Studies**

58.   Jon Mills and Janusz A. Polanowski, *The Ontology of Prejudice.* A volume in **Philosophy and Psychology**

59.   Leena Vilkka, *The Intrinsic Value of Nature*

60.   Palmer Talbutt, Jr., Rough Dialectics: *Sorokin's Philosophy of Value*, with contributions by Lawrence T. Nichols and Pitirim A. Sorokin

61.   C. L. Sheng, *A Utilitarian General Theory of Value*

62.   George David Miller, *Negotiating Toward Truth: The Extinction of Teachers and Students*. Epilogue by Mark Roelof Eleveld.
A volume in **Philosophy of Education**

63.   William Gerber, *Love, Poetry, and Immortality: Luminous Insights of the World's Great Thinkers*

64.   Dane R. Gordon, Editor, *Philosophy in Post-Communist Europe*.
A volume in **Post-Communist European Thought**

65.   Dane R. Gordon and Józef Niznik, Editors, *Criticism and Defense of Rationality in Contemporary Philosophy*.
A volume in **Post-Communist European Thought**

66.   John R. Shook, *Pragmatism: An Annotated Bibliography, 1898-1940*. With contributions by E. Paul Colella, Lesley Friedman, Frank X. Ryan, and Ignas K. Skrupskelis

67.   Lansana Keita, *The Human Project and the Temptations of Science*

68.   Michael M. Kazanjian*, Phenomenology and Education: Cosmology, Co-Being, and Core Curriculum*. A volume in **Philosophy of Education**

69.   James W. Vice, *The Reopening of the American Mind: On Skepticism and Constitutionalism*

70.   Sarah Bishop Merrill, *Defining Personhood: Toward the Ethics of Quality in Clinical Care*

71.   Dane R. Gordon, *Philosophy and Vision*

72.   Alan Milchman and Alan Rosenberg, Editors, *Postmodernism and the Holocaust*. A volume in **Holocaust and Genocide Studies**

73.   Peter A. Redpath, *Masquerade of the Dream Walkers: Prophetic Theology from the Cartesians to Hegel*. A volume in **Studies in the History of Western**

Philosophy

74. Malcolm D. Evans, *Whitehead and Philosophy of Education: The Seamless Coat of Learning*. A volume in **Philosophy of Education**

75. Warren E. Steinkraus, *Taking Religious Claims Seriously: A Philosophy of Religion*, edited by Michael H. Mitias. A volume in **Universal Justice**

76. Thomas Magnell, Editor, *Values and Education*

77. Kenneth A. Bryson, *Persons and Immortality*. A volume in **Natural Law Studies**

78. Steven V. Hicks, *International Law and the Possibility of a Just World Order: An Essay on Hegel's Universalism*. A volume in **Universal Justice**

79. E. F. Kaelin, *Texts on Texts and Textuality: A Phenomenology of Literary Art*, Edited by Ellen J. Burns

80. Amihud Gilead, Saving Possibilities: A Study in Philosophical Psychology. *A volume in Philosophy and Psychology*

81. André Mineau, *The Making of the Holocaust: Ideology and Ethics in the Systems Perspective*. A volume in **Holocaust and Genocide Studies**

82. Howard P. Kainz, *Politically Incorrect Dialogues: Topics Not Discussed in Polite Circles*

83. Veikko Launis, Juhani Pietarinen, and Juha Räikkä, Editors, *Genes and Morality: New Essays*. A volume in **Nordic Value Studies**

84. Steven Schroeder, *The Metaphysics of Cooperation: A Study of F. D. Maurice*

85. Caroline Joan ("Kay") S. Picart, *Thomas Mann and Friedrich Nietzsche: Eroticism, Death, Music, and Laughter*. A volume in **Central-European Value Studies**

86. G. John M. Abbarno, Editor, *The Ethics of Homelessness: Philosophical Perspectives*

AA0-9904